1901–P

e Day
Martin Collier • Rosemary Rees
Series editors: Martin Collier • Rosemary Rees

Planning and Resource Pack 3

www.heinemann.co.uk
✓ Free online support
✓ Useful weblinks
✓ 24 hour online ordering

01865 888080

Heinemann is an imprint of Pearson Education Limited, a company incorporated in England and Wales, having its registered office at Edinburgh Gate, Harlow, Essex, CM20 2JE. Registered company number: 872828

www.heinemann.co.uk

Heinemann is a registered trademark of Pearson Education Limited

Text © Pearson Education Limited 2009

First published 2009

12 11 10 09 08
10 9 8 7 6 5 4 3 2 1

British Library Cataloguing in Publication Data
A catalogue record for this book is available from the British Library

ISBN 978 0 435319 02 1

Copyright notice
All rights reserved. The material in this publication is copyright. Pupil sheets may be freely photocopied for classroom use in the purchasing institution. However, this material is copyright and under no circumstances may copies be offered for sale. If you wish to use the material in any way other than that specified you must apply in writing to the publisher. Applications for the copyright owner's written permission should be addressed to the publisher.

Edited and Proofread by Rosie Bird
Typeset by AT Communication
Original illustrations © Pearson Education Ltd 2009
Illustrated by Tek Art
Picture research by Elena Goodinson
Cover photo © The Bridgman Art Library/ Christie's Images
Printed in the UK by Ashford Colour Press Limited

Acknowledgements
The author and publisher would like to thank the following individuals and organisations for permission to reproduce photographs:
Worksheet 2.2b © Lincolnshire Archives; Worksheet 3.2c(1) © Imperial War Museum; Worksheet 3.2c(3) © Imperial War Museum

Every effort has been made to contact copyright holders of material reproduced in this book. Any omissions will be rectified in subsequent printings if notice is given to the publishers.

Websites
There are links to relevant websites in this book. In order to ensure that the links are up to date, that the links work, and that the sites are not inadvertently linked to sites that could be considered offensive, we have made the links available on the Heinemann website at www.heinemann.co.uk/hotlinks. When you access the site, the express code is 9021T.

Contents

Introduction
Introduction 4
Overview of *History in Progress 3* 10

Unit 1 Ruling
1.1 What did the suffragettes do to get the vote? 18
1.2 How did one assassination cause a war? 22
1.3 How was the First World War fought? 26
1.4 What was the impact of the end of the First World War? 34
1.5 What were the key moments of the Second World War? 39
1.6 How did governments respond after the Second World War? 45
1.7 Who had an impact in the struggle for civil rights in the USA? 51
1.8 How can you respond to terrorism? 54
1.9 Making Connections 60
1.10 Assessment 1 63
1.11 Assessment 2 68

Unit 2 Living and Working
2.1 Was there truly an Edwardian 'Golden Summer'? 69
2.2 How were the 'home fires' kept burning during the First World War? 73
2.3 How did people in Britain survive the Second World War? 79
2.4 Why do genocides happen? 87
2.5 Where was life better in the 1930s: communist Russia or capitalist America? 96
2.6 How did Chairman Mao change China? 101
2.7 Did the Cold War lead to an age of fear? 106
2.8 How did healthcare change in the twentieth century? 110
2.9 What was it like 'back in my day…'? 114
2.10 What role did Trade Unions play in people's lives? 116
2.11 Making Connections 120
2.12 Assessment 1 121
2.13 Assessment 2 125

Unit 3 Moving and Travelling
3.1 Who answered the call to war? 127
3.2 How can moving make you safe? 130
3.3 How did the British rule in India come to an end? 139
3.4 Why did people leave their homelands? 143
3.5 How did African colonies gain independence? 149
3.6 Where can migration lead? 154
3.7 Making Connections 156
3.8 Assessment 1 158
3.9 Assessment 2 161

Introduction

Rationale behind the course

History in Progress has been written to help teachers deliver the requirements of the revised History National Curriculum Key Stage 3 Programme of Study. The course incorporates all of the new strands included in the revised Programme of Study including an emphasis on enquiry and diversity. History in Progress is a course devised for pupils studying in the twenty-first century.

History in Progress has been planned and written with the following wider curriculum and school issues in mind.

- The individual child comes first. *History in Progress* takes into account the priorities from the *Every Child Matters* agenda by providing for the individuals' needs, through a range of well-structured tasks and focused success criteria in every lesson.

- The course caters for a very broad range of pupils' abilities. There is clear differentiation through both task and outcome providing an appropriate challenge to learners of all abilities. The books and assessment tasks are structured in such a way so as to provide stretch and challenge for all learners, not just the most able.

- *History in Progress* has been structured to facilitate the aims of the Secondary National Strategy to deliver teaching and learning of the highest quality. Each enquiry is focused on specific learning objectives, with clear outcomes based on the principles of 'All … Most … Some …'.

- The course is flexible, providing a variety of pathways through the Key Stage 3 History curriculum.

- It is understood that there is time constraint on the amount of time given to History at Key Stage 3 so *History in Progress* provides opportunities for the delivery of History through cross-curricular initiatives as well as a distinct discipline.

- It has been devised with the classroom of the twenty-first century in mind and takes full account of changing technologies, both in terms of delivery of the course and pupils' work. There are ICT links built in throughout the course to help pupils process data research information and successfully present their findings.

- Citizenship is an important element of the curriculum. *History in Progress* provides opportunities to deliver Citizenship through a historical context, both in terms of content and pupils' skills.

- *History in Progress* promotes a variety of learning approaches. There is an emphasis on individualised learning, problem solving and discovery. There are also opportunities in every enquiry for visual and kinaesthetic learning. Additionally, pupils encouraged to work in pairs and groups, and a range of strategies are suggested throughout this Planning and Resource Pack to allow for this.

- The course has been devised to promote tolerance and diversity both through its content and the learning processes.

- The Pupil Book is complemented by detailed lesson plans in the Planning and Resource Pack, which have been designed so that the lessons can be delivered by either a subject specialist or a non-subject specialist.

- *History in Progress* aims to enhance the pupils' literacy and communication skills through activities that encourage a range of outcomes – speaking, role play, extended writing, presentations, debate.

History in Progress was planned and written to address the following History-specific issues.

- The course provides overview alongside opportunity for the study of history in themes and in depth.

- It has been devised with the aim of promoting pupil interest in and enthusiasm for History.

- The content of the course and the ways in which that content is tackled aims to make History relevant to all pupils.

- It is hoped that following the *History in Progress* scheme will provide the impetus for pupils to opt to continue to study History at Key Stage 4.

- Through introducing meaningful cross-cultural links and the cross-curricular initiatives outlined earlier, *History in Progress* attempts to instil a greater understanding of context and a greater sense of period.

- Throughout the course, there is a greater emphasis on source work as part of a wider historical enquiry as recommended by the Historical Association 14–19 Curriculum Report.

- The course promotes chronological understanding and encourages pupils to build a chronological framework of periods studied in which new knowledge can be contextualised.

- Pupils are encouraged to identify and explain change and continuity within and across periods of history and are presented with ample opportunities to analyse and explain the reasons for and results of historical events, situations and changes.
- *History in Progress* aims to provide clarity around historical interpretations and significance in history, providing enquiries that allow pupils to focus on these concepts.
- Pupils are encouraged to make links and connections between topics of study both within and across time periods, countries and themes.

Key features of *History in Progress*

History

The aim of *History in Progress* is to make History both attractive and relevant to pupils. The enquiries have been selected and written with the aim of stimulating the pupils' imagination, thereby drawing them in to the subject. History is and must remain relevant to young people. *History in Progress* aims to bring History alive so that pupils can identify with the subject.

The history in the series looks at the past from a range of perspectives. It balances the study of national and international affairs with a focus on the personal and the local. The series shows through comparison and a broad perspective that all history needs to be understood in a wider context; that the history of a locality cannot be fully grasped without an understanding of the larger national and international context.

The series also aims to draw the pupils into the process of history. The enquiries have been designed in such a way that the pupils will understand that history is a discipline based on enquiry, interpretation and decision-making. It is hoped that pupils will understand that the process of history relies on discussion and debate.

History in Progress has been written to help prepare pupils for life after school. From the start of the series, it emphasises the diversity and fluidity of society hundreds of years ago. The series promotes citizenship, both in terms of the history studied but also the processes of debate, negotiation and voting that are integral to a number of the activities. The series stresses the historical diversity of the national community and the links and interdependence within the international community.

Structure

The curriculum has been structured through the combination of the key concepts, key processes and identified areas of study. The Programme of Study suggests a number of areas of study. These have been rationalised into three defining themes of study:

- Ruling
- Living and working
- Moving and travelling.

Through studying all units, the pupils are working through the key concepts identified in the revised Programme of Study – see pages 12–17. They gain extensive experience of working with evidence as part of an historical enquiry and communicating their ideas in a clear and structured fashion.

Unit 1: Ruling

This unit focuses on the ways in which power was exercised in the twentieth and early twenty-first centuries, and on the ways in which people tried to acquire power. The unit is broken up into enquiries that are set out in a broadly chronological framework. The enquiries focus predominantly on the two world wars, how they were fought and their impact. There is the opportunity to investigate how individuals attempted to empower not only themselves but their wider community, and here the suffragettes in Britain and Rosa Parks in the US provide the focus. The Unit ends with a consideration of the abuse of power by exploring acts of terrorism world-wide, asks what terrorism is about and how we should respond to it.

Unit 2: Living and working

This unit explores in detail the changes that took place in people's everyday lives during this period. It begins by considering everyday life in Britain before 1914 and during the two world wars. It looks beyond Britain by investigating two major genocides: the Holocaust and the killings in Rwanda. Life in communist Russia and capitalist America in the 1930s is considered, compared and contrasted, and the changes Mao brought to China are investigated. The impact of the Cold War on people's lives forms the focus of another series of enquiries as does the positive impact of improvements in healthcare world-wide. The Unit ends by returning to Britain and looking at everyday life in the 1950s and 60s and at the impact of trade unions on working lives.

Unit 3: Moving and travelling

This unit is underpinned by the unprecedented

Introduction

movement of peoples during this period. The main movements of people considered in macro and micro enquiries focus on the upheavals of war, decolonisation, immigration and emigration. Enquiries focus on a wide range of diverse events, from Kindertransport to African decolonisation, from Indian Independence to *Windrush*. The Unit ends by a consideration of the journey of one family from Kenya to the White House: Barack Obama.

Carefully levelled tasks

Each enquiry includes a progression of colour-coded tasks. The colouring of each task is so that teachers and pupils can identify the national curriculum level. This system has been designed to facilitate ongoing assessment and effective tracking of the pupils' progress.

Different levels of tasks are offered to promote pupil choice and encourage them to select their own individual learning pathways. The system can also be used to challenge all pupils to work at a higher level.

This is the key to the colour coding throughout the *History in Progress* series.

	Year 7	Year 8	Year 9
Green tasks	level 4	level 4/5	level 5
Blue tasks	level 4/5	level 5	level 5/6
Orange tasks	level 5	level 5/6	level 6
Purple tasks	level 5/6	level 6	level 7

Taking it further!

'Taking it further!' features within the Pupil Books provide pupils with further stretch and challenge and can be used in a number of ways:

- as extension work in class
- as distinct lessons for more able classes
- as homework exercises to build on skills, knowledge and concepts learned in class.

Some 'Taking it further!' sections attempt to deal with controversies and provoke discussion and debate. Others enquires have been left open to encourage further research work and independent learning.

Back to the start

At the end of the many of the enquiries, 'Back to the start' can be used to serve a number of purposes.

- It can be used as part of the plenary to direct pupils' attention back to the main themes.

- In some cases it directs pupils to reflect on overarching concepts that cover more than one enquiry.

'Back to the start' can be used to encourage pupils to reflect not only on the content covered but also on the processes undertaken and the skills practised through the course of the enquiry.

Making connections

'Making connections', at the end of each unit, draw together some of the dominant themes in that unit. They can be used as whole lessons, and lesson plans are provided in the Planning and Resource Pack.

Alternatively, the 'Making connections' exercises can be used as the starting point for a research project that allows pupils to explore the identified themes and concepts in greater detail.

Skillsbank

A 'Skillsbank' has been provided at the end of the Pupil Book; it can be used in several different ways:

- to provide support for pupils needing additional practice in specific skills
- to enable pupils to extend their range of skills-based understandings and competencies
- to add to the range of accessible homework tasks
- to provide a point of reference for pupils working individually or in groups
- to enable development of those skills targeted by GCSE History examinations.

Assessment

Accurate and effective assessment is a central component of *History in Progress*. Indeed, an opportunity for assessment of the pupils' progress is integrated into every enquiry. The course encourages a balance of formal assessment, through the inclusion of assessment tasks at the end of each unit, and ongoing informal assessment.

Such informal assessment is an essential component in the tracking of pupil progress and recognition of an individual's improved performance. It will help in identifying each pupil's strengths and weaknesses and will inform strategies for further progress. It will also help teachers to set individual targets for pupils.

Teachers are not expected to provide a level for every piece of work. However, the innovative assessment structure provided by *History in Progress* through the colour-coded, levelled tasks enables the teacher to quickly and accurately judge levels of current performance.

The formal and informal assessment tasks completed throughout each unit will provide teachers with the evidence to support an overall judgement as to the level of each pupil's performance.

The assessment tasks in each unit explain the tasks clearly, provide instructions on what pupils should do, and offer hints, tips and suggestions to get them started. Further support is provided in the accompanying teacher notes in the Planning and Resource Pack. The markschemes in the Planning and Resource Pack provide a pupil-friendly approach to assessing their work, and encourage target setting and reflection.

Peer- and self-assessment

There are opportunities throughout the course for peer and self assessment. Plenaries in particular have been designed to encourage self-review not only of knowledge but also of how pupils have learned and participated in the lesson. Below is a list suggestions for including pupils in the assessment process.

- Provide opportunities for pupils to respond to teacher and peer marking.
- Give them a chance to assess their own work before the teacher.
- Provide opportunities for analysis of existing markschemes.
- Encourage pupils to devise their own markschemes for activities.

Learning strategies

Thinking skills throughout History in Progress

A wide variety of different approaches to the development of thinking skills is provided throughout History in Progress. Pupils are invited to explore, examine and investigate, to empathise, appreciate, debate and reflect. The ways in which these essential thinking skills can be developed further are suggested in the Planning and Resource Pack. Although, here, these skills are history orientated, they are transferable to other subjects and disciplines.

Think pair share

Many of the tasks in *History in Progress 3* can be carried out in this way. This approach ensures that all pupils have had chance to consider their response to a question. They will have already thought about it and tried it out on their partner and should be able to answer if asked by the teacher. This strategy can also eliminate the need for hands up, as asking for answers from a range of pupils is likely to result in a range of considered responses.

Snowballing

This is a way to encourage sharing of ideas and development of response among pupils. Pose a question or suggest a discussion point and ask pupils to work individually to record their response. They then work with a partner to develop a shared response, then in a group of four to develop a common answer, and so on as appropriate. At each stage they should incorporate the best ideas from the previous responses, thus encouraging ongoing reflection and refinement of the ideas. Take whole-class feedback when the group work has been completed.

Gimme 5

The aim of this is for pupils to recall information and recap learning. As pupils come in the classroom ask them to write five ideas connected to a particular topic. These can then be shared in pairs, groups or with the whole class.

Quick-fire questions

A useful starter activity, this can be used to recap learning from a previous lesson before moving on to develop that knowledge and understanding. Prepare a list of questions, preferably with short answers, on a topic and go round the class asking for responses. Pupils should aim to keep their answers as short and to the point as possible and to respond quickly to the question. Alternatively, you could ask pupils to prepare questions that can then be asked by either the teacher or by the pupil.

Vote with your feet

Pupils position themselves by moving to stand along a continuum, across the classroom or along one wall, to show their opinion about a subject or their strength of feeling for or against a particular question or issue. This can be done once, when new information is introduced, and then done again to see whether pupils have, literally, shifted their position.

Mysteries

Mysteries (e.g. **Lesson 2.1c** Great Fire of London: accident or arson?) that focus around a key question can be used to develop problem-solving skills. Pupils have to evaluate a range of evidence and possible responses and suggest a solution to the problem. They are an effective way of involving pupils in higher order thinking skills such as classification,

Introduction

speculation and testing hypotheses. In a reversal of roles, you might want to ask pupils to devise their own mysteries, coming up with a key question connected to a topic they have been studying and then suggesting evidence for analysis either from *History in Progress* or other sources.

Differentiation

Differentiation is provided in a variety of different ways to be used as appropriate.

- **Differentiation by task** is encouraged by the use of colour-coded tasks linked to specific levels. Lower achievers are supported by the provision, in the Planning and Resource Pack, of writing frames and thinking grids. The 'Taking it further!' sections provide stretch and challenge for the more able pupils. Again, the use of these is further supported by the Planning and Resource Pack.
- **Differentiation by outcome** is enabled by the provision of 'levelled' markschemes. These have been written in a pupil-friendly way so that peer review and individual challenge are both possible ways of assessing pupil achievement. The Planning and Resource Pack provides appropriate grids for pupils to complete that enable them to reflect on their achievement and progress and to consider what they have to do to move up within a level or move up a complete level.

Cross-curricular links

Many of the enquiries can provide cross-curricular links and these can be developed by the teacher if appropriate within the curriculum of individual schools.

Subject	Examples of linking lessons
PSHE	1.4d, 2.2a,b
Citizenship	1.1a, 1.2a, 1.4c, 1.7c, 2.4a
RE	3.2a,b,d .3.3b
English	1.3, 2.3b, 2.11
Geography	1.8b, 2.2c

Inclusion

The *History in Progress* course is designed to provide effective learning opportunities for all pupils.

The layout of each unit, the use of pictures and colour-coding and the staged assessment tasks are all designed to make the series accessible to all pupils. The choice of content in the course has been made in such a way as to enhance the recognition of cultural diversity as something of value for all learners. The range of tasks and variety of design and layout are offered in such a way as to cater for pupils with different learning styles. The approaches to teaching and learning will motivate pupils of both genders from different social backgrounds.

History in Progress is supported by a Planning and Resource Pack that includes worksheets that can be used to support learners with specific learning difficulties. The 'Taking it further!' features aim to stretch and engage the more able learners but can be used to provide all pupils with alternative activities as appropriate.

The use of ICT and the ICT support materials further ensure that the course is open to all learners.

Using ICT

There are opportunities throughout *History in Progress* for pupils to use ICT to support and extend their learning. It can be used as an information source, to search for and select relevant information and evidence, and to present and refine their work. Many of the activities lend themselves to ICT ranging from the use of Word or PowerPoint to present written work to the use of Microsoft Publisher to create posters and displays.

Suggestions for further research using the Internet have been made throughout the Planning and Resource Pack in the lesson plans. However, it is important that pupils develop skills that enable them to review information from the internet critically.

The LiveText CD-ROM that accompanies each Pupil Book contains a wide variety of additional activities and models that will enhance pupils' thinking and learning in History.

Local history

An important element of the new National Curriculum History is a focus on local history. It is important that pupils have an opportunity to investigate local history as part of their Key Stage 3 studies. Engagement with local sources and visits to local sites of significance are fundamental in helping the pupils appreciate the relevance of the past to their own lives.

History in Progress has been designed in such a way to stimulate the delivery of local history. The course is structured in a way that gives teachers and pupils the opportunity to explore the history of their localities.

There are plenty of opportunities in *History in Progress* for pupils to engage in local history. These are some examples:

The emphasis placed on the two world wars could lead to a research project centred on the ways in which a particular area, town or village coped. The pupils could research local recruitment and the various different ways in which people on the Home Front coped. The Home Front in the First and Second World Wars could be compared and contrasted, using local records. The enquiry could start with local war memorials and the research can then continue from these into exploring the different experiences of the families of the men recorded on the memorials. Local ex-servicemen's' clubs could prove to be a rich resource, as could regimental records. Students should be reminded to focus sharply on the Home Front or on the experiences of the fighting forces.

In a similar way, students could explore the activities of suffragettes and suffragists in their region. How much activity was there? Where was it recorded? What part did women play in local life?

Schools situated in an area where there is an immigrant community could tap into this community in order to provide an enhanced understanding of the problems faced by an immigrant community and of the richness they provide to the locality. Local links here will be of vital importance.

The above suggestions are just examples. There is considerable scope for other local history enquiries. Pupils might be encouraged to investigate the history of migration into their locality. This might include inviting representatives of immigrant communities into their schools to tell pupils the history of their community and answer questions.

Setting up an enquiry

As part of their work at Key Stage 3, pupils should be encouraged set up and follow their own structured enquiries. History in Progress provides a range of opportunities for pupils to do this.

- Before setting up an enquiry, make sure that pupils understand the terms and conditions of the enquiry with regards to structure, subject content and possible outcomes.

- Ensure that pupils are clear about how to devise questions that will form the basis of an hypothesis. One way of devising these questions is to use a statement followed by question stems such as 'To what extent do you agree with this statement?' or 'How far do you agree with this statement?' (See text that follows.)

- Advise pupils on where they might find relevant and appropriate information for their research. They should be encouraged to use reference books, the Internet, visit the school or local library.

- As in any enquiry, encourage pupils to consider both sides of a hypothesis before coming to their conclusion. As part of the conclusion, pupils should outline the evidence that supports either side before coming to a conclusion.

- The outcome to an enquiry can be presented in a number of ways from through written work, wall displays or as oral presentations.

What question shall I ask?

Once pupils have read through the information they should then attempt to set up an enquiry. This is best done through the asking of questions

Exemplar enquiry

Here is an example of a set enquiry that has come out of one of the units in *History in Progress* Book 3. Pupils have been set the following task, based on a study of the information in the Enquiries to find out what it would have been like to have been a child in 20th century Britain. Here, it is important that the students themselves select the appropriate enquiries. Clearly some are sharply focused on Britain; others could well be used for their peripheral impact.

After considering the above issue, the pupils have then suggested the following hypothesis:

'It was better to be a child in 1920 than in 1950.'

To what extent do you agree with this statement?

Overview of History in Progress – Book 3 (Year 9)

The following grid outlines how *History in Progress – Book 3* has been designed to provide full support for the Programme of Study.

Enquiry	Chronological focus	Lessons	Key concepts and processes NB Process 2.3 *Communicating about the Past* permeates all lessons	Content	Cross-curriculum dimensions
Unit 1 Ruling					
1.1 What did the suffragettes do to get the vote?	1900–18	a) Were the suffragettes right to use violence?	1.4 Cause/consequence 2.2a, b Using evidence	3d, g	Citizenship
		b) Emily Davison: suicide or accident?	1.4 Cause/consequence 2.1a,b Historical enquiry 2.2a,b Using evidence	3d	
1.2 How did one assassination cause a war?	1908–14	a) Why did war break out in the Balkans?	1.1b,c Chronological understanding 1.4 Cause / consequence 2.2a,b Using evidence	3j	Citizenship
		b) How did a world war begin?	1.1c Chronological understanding 1.4 Cause / consequence	3j	
1.3 How was the First World War fought?	1914–18	a) We want to volunteer!	1.2 Diversity 2.2 Using evidence	3g, j	Citizenship PSHE English
		b) What was life like on the front line?	1.2 Diversity 2.1a,b Historical enquiry 2.2a,b Using evidence	3g, j	
		c) What happened on the first day of the Battle of the Somme?	1.6b Interpretation 2.1a,b Historical enquiry 2.2a,b Using evidence	3g, j	
		d) Why were soldiers shot at dawn?	1.2 Diversity 2.1a,b Historical enquiry 2.2a, b Using evidence	3g, j	
		e) Remembering the war	1.5 Significance 2.1a,b Historical enquiry 2.2a,b Using evidence	3g, j	

Overview of History in Progress 3

				Citizenship PSHE
1.4 What was the impact of the end of the First World War?	1919-39	a) A land fit for heroes?	1.3 Change/continuity; 2.1a Historical enquiry	3g
		b) What was the reaction in Germany to the end of the war?	1.5 Significance; 2.2a,b Using evidence	3i, j
		c) How was the League of Nations perceived?	1.5 Significance; 1.6c Interpretation; 2.2a,b Using evidence	3j
		d) Was appeasement the right policy?	1.4 Cause and consequence; 1.5 Significance; 2.1b Historical enquiry	3g, i, j
1.5 What were the key moments of the Second World War?	1939-45	a) Dunkirk: victory or defeat?	1.4 Cause/consequence	3i	Global dimension Identity and cultural diversity
		b) Pearl Harbour: what is the story?	1.5 Significance; 1.6c Interpretations	3i
		c) What was the significance of Stalingrad?	1.4 Cause/consequence	3i
		d) Questions for Martha	1.5 Significance; 1.6c Interpretations	3i
		e) Hiroshima: use of the bomb, right or wrong?	1.6a, b, c Interpretations; 2.2a, b Evidence	3i
1.6 How did governments respond after the Second World War?		a) Has the United Nations helped to create a better world?	1.4 Cause/consequence; 2.1a, 2.1b Enquiry; 2.3b Communicating	3d	Community participation
		b) Why did it take sixteen years for Britain to join the European Community?	1.6a Interpretation; 2.2b Evidence; 2.3a Communicating	3d
		c) Devolution: what's in it for us?	1.4a Cause/consequence; 2.1b Enquiry; 2.3b Communicating	3d

Overview of History in Progress 3

1.7 Who had an impact in the struggle for civil rights in the USA?	1860–1968	a) How did Rosa Parks transform America?	1.3 Change and continuity 1.4 Cause and consequence 2.1b Historical enquiry	3i	Citizenship
		b) Why was Malcolm X assassinated?	1.2 Diversity 2.1a,b Historical enquiry 2.2a,b Using evidence	3i	
		c) Why was Martin Luther King seen as a threat?	1.5 Significance 2.2a,b Using evidence	3i	
1.8 How can you respond to terrorism?	1943–present	a) Why is Tamerlan Satsayev afraid to go to school?	1.2 Diversity 1.4 Cause and consequence 2.1a,b Historical enquiry	3i	Citizenship Geography Media
		b) Nelson Mandela: activist or terrorist?	1.2 Diversity 1.4 Cause and consequence 2.1a,b Historical enquiry	3i, j	
		c) Why should we learn about terrorism?	1.4 Cause and consequence 1.6b Interpretation 2.1a,b Historical enquiry	3i	
		d) Ireland 1966–1997: why did 'the Troubles' last so long?	1.1a,b,c Chronological understanding 1.3 Change and continuity 1.4 Cause and consequence	3e	
		e) Is there any solution to terrorism?	1.3 Change and continuity 1.4 Cause and consequence 2.1b Historical enquiry	3g, i	
1.9 Making connections		Who had the most effect?	1.5 Significance		
1.10 Assessment 1		Why have their been different interpretations of Lenin?	1.6a, b, c Interpretations; 2.2a, b Using evidence 2.3 Communicating about the past		
1.11 Assessment 2		Who had the most success in changing the way people were ruled in the twentieth century?	1.5 Significance 2.1b Historical enquiry 2.3 Communicating about the past		

Overview of History in Progress 3

Unit 2 Living and working					
2.1 Was there truly an Edwardian 'golden summer'?	1900–14	a) What was life like for the Upper Class?	1.2 Diversity 2.2a, b Using evidence	3g	Citizenship
		b) Threats to Stability	1.5 Significance 2.1a, b Historical enquiry	3g	
2.2 How were the 'home fires' kept burning during the First World War?	1914–18	a) How did the country keep going?	1.2 Diversity; 1.3 Change/continuity 2.2a Using evidence	3g	PSHE Economic awareness
		b) What did people fear?	1.2 Diversity 1.4 Cause and consequence 2.2b Using evidence	3g	Citizenship Geography
		c) Did everyone in Britain hate the Germans?	1.2 Diversity 2.2b Using evidence	3g	
2.3 How did people in Britain survive the Second World War?	1939–45	a) What did people fear this time?	1.2 Diversity 1.4 Cause and consequence 1.6c Interpretations 2.2a Using evidence	3g	English PSHE
		b) How were children kept safe?	1.2 Diversity 1.4 Cause and consequence 2.2a,b Using evidence	3g	
		c) How were people fed?	1.3 Change and continuity 1.4 Cause and consequence 2.2b Using evidence	3g	
		d) The end of the war in Europe	1.2 Diversity 2.2b Using evidence	3g	

Overview of History in Progress 3

2.4 Why do genocides happen?	1939-1994	a) How did the Nazis try to kill all European Jews?	1.2 Diversity 1.5 Significance 2.2a,b Using evidence	3i, j	Citizenship PSHE
		b) Who was to blame for the 'Final Solution'?	1.4 Cause and consequence 1.5 Significance 1.6a,b Interpretations 2.1a,b Historical enquiry 2.2a,b Using evidence	3j	
		c) Why did the Hutus try to kill all the Tutsis?	1.4 cause and consequence 1.5 Significance; 2.1a,b Historical enquiry 2.2a,b Using evidence	3h	
		d) Are genocides unique?	1.3 Change and continuity 1.4 Cause and consequence 1.5 Significance	3i	
2.5 Where was life better in the 1930s: communist Russia or capitalist America?	1930-39	a) What was life like in the USA in the 1930s?	1.3 Change and continuity 1.4 Cause and consequence 2.2a,b Using evidence	3i	Citizenship PSHE
		b) What was life like in the USSR in the 1930s?	1.3 Change and continuity 1.4 Cause and consequence 1.6a Interpretation 2.2a,b Using evidence	3i	
2.6 How did Chairman Mao change China?	1949-68	a) What was the Great Leap Forward?	1.2 Diversity 1.3 Change and continuity 2.2a,b Using evidence	3i	Citizenship
		b) What was the Cultural Revolution?	1.2 Diversity 1.4 Cause and consequence 2.2a,b Using evidence	3i	

Overview of History in Progress 3

2.7 Did the Cold War lead to an age of fear?	1945–90	a) What was the Cold War?	1.3 Change and continuity 1.4 Cause and consequence 1.5 Significance	3i, j	Geography Citizenship Media Science
		b) Living in the shadow of the bomb: Cuba	1.4 Cause and consequence 1.5 Significance 2.1a,b Historical enquiry 2.2a,b Using evidence	3i, j	
		c) How to survive a nuclear attack	1.4 Cause and consequence 2.2a,b Using evidence	3i, j	
		d) Life behind the wall	1.2 Diversity 1.5 Significance 2.2a, b Using evidence	3i	
2.8 How did healthcare change in the twentieth century?	1900–present	a) Which was the greatest breakthrough in healthcare?	1.3 Change and continuity 1.4 Cause and consequence 1.5 Significance 2.2b Using evidence	3g	Science Media Citizenship
		b) Out with the old; in with the new?	1.3 Change and continuity 1.4 Cause and consequence 1.5 Significance	3g	Citizenship
2.9 What was it like 'back in my day ….'?	1950–60	a) You've never had it so good: Britain in the 1950s	1.3 Change and continuity 1.5 Significance 2.2a,b Historical enquiry 2.2a,b Using evidence	3d, 3g	
		b) Growing up in the 1960s	2.1a, b Enquiry	3d, 3g	
2.10 What role did trade unions play in people's lives?	1904–85	a) Why join a union?	1.1b Chronology; 2.3b Communicating	3d, g	PSHE Citizenship
		b) Why did miners strike?	2.1a, b Enquiry	3d, 3h	
2.11 Making connections		Twentieth century Exhibition	1.2 Diversity 2.2a,b Using evidence		
2.12 Assessment 1		Was it better to be a child in 1918, 1955 or 2005?	1.3 Change and continuity 2.3 Communicating about the past		

Schemes of work

2.13 Assessment 2		What was life like in the twentieth century?	1.5 Significance 1.6c Interpretation 2.2a,b Using evidence 2.3 Communicating about the past	
Unit 3 Moving and travelling				
3.1 Who answered the call to war?	1914–18	a) For king and country, 1914–18?	1.4 Cause and consequence 2.1a,b Historical enquiry 2.2a,b Using evidence	3g Citizenship
		b) What was the reaction in Britain to the arrival of Empire troops?	1.2 Diversity 1.4 Cause and consequence 2.2b Using evidence	3g
3.2 How can moving make you safe?	1939–47	a) What was Kindertransport?	1.2 Diversity 1.4 Cause and consequence 2.1a,b Historical enquiry 2.2a,b Using evidence	3f, j Citizenship Religious Studies English
		b) What motivated Oskar Schindler?	1.4 Cause and consequence 1.6b Interpretation 2.1b Historical enquiry 2.2b Using evidence	3i, j
		c) Adam Rybczynski's story	1.1 Chronological understanding 1.4 Cause and consequence 2.1b Historical enquiry 2.2b Using evidence	3i, j
		d) What was Exodus 1947?	1.4 Cause and consequence 2.1b Historical enquiry 2.2a,b Using evidence	3i, j
3.3 How did the British rule in India come to an end?	1947–8	a) Why did the British leave India in 1947?	1.3 Change and continuity 1.4 Cause and consequence	3h, i, j Citizenship PSHE
		b) Why did 12 million Indians leave their homes in 1947?	1.3 Change and continuity 1.4 Cause and consequence 2.2b Using evidence	3h, i, j Religious Studies

Schemes of work

3.4 Why did people leave their homelands?	a) What effect did the arrival of the SS *Empire Windrush* have?	1.2 Diversity 1.3 Change and continuity 1.4 Cause and consequence 2.2a,b Using evidence	3h, i	Citizenship PSHE
	b) British and Asian: a clash of cultures?	1.2 Diversity 1.3 Change and continuity 2.2b Historical enquiry	3h, i	
	c) Why were British children sent to Australia?	1.4 Cause and consequence 2.2a, b Using evidence	3g, h	
3.5 How did African colonies gain independence?	a) Does Kwame Nkrumah deserve to be remembered as the 'Osagyefo' of Ghana?	1.3 Change and continuity 1.4 Cause and consequence	3h, i	Citizenship
	b) Why did the Algerians fight for their freedom?	1.3 Change and continuity 1.4 Cause and consequence	3i	
	c) Who is to blame for the problems in Zimbabwe?	1.3 Change and continuity 1.4 Cause and consequence 2.1a,b Historical enquiry	3i	
3.6 Where can migration lead?	a) Why move from Africa to Hawaii?	1.3 Change and continuity 1.4 Cause and consequence 1.6b Interpretation	3i	Citizenship English Geography
	b) A long road to the White House	1.1 Chronological understanding 1.2 Diversity 1.3 Change and continuity 1.4 Cause and consequence	3i	
3.7 Making connections	Why did people move around in the twentieth century?	2.1a,b Historical enquiry		
3.8 Assessment 1	Why did people travel in the twentieth century?	1.4 Cause and consequence 2.2a,b Using evidence 2.3 Communicating about the past		
3.9 Assessment 2	What was the most important movement of people in the twentieth century?	1.5 Significance 2.3 Communicating about the past		

> 1 Ruling

1.1 What did the suffragettes do to get the vote?

1.1a Were the suffragettes right to use violence?

Learning objectives
- To find out about the methods used by the suffragettes.
- To investigate reactions to the suffragettes of those in authority.

Historical background

In 1897, the various groups in the UK that supported votes for women came together as the National Union of Women's Suffrage Societies (NUWSS) led by Millicent Fawcett. They aimed to use constitutional methods to bring about change. Despite many debates and growing support for female enfranchisement in the Commons, their bills did not have government support. In 1903, irritated by the lack of progress, Emmeline Pankhurst and her daughter Christabel set up the Women's Social and Political Union (WSPU). Their methods to bring votes for women to public attention were confrontational and often illegal. Many argue that they harmed, rather than furthered, the women's cause.

Teaching Activities and Learning Outcomes

Assessment opportunity

Making links between actions and outcomes.

Pupils will be able to

- study a photograph and work in pairs to develop questioning about what it shows
- consider evidence to reach a conclusion
- empathise with suffragettes and the victims of their activities.

Starter

Ask the whole class to stand up. Tell all the girls that because they cannot vote, they must now sit down (female staff in the room should sit down too, including the teacher). For every ten boys that are standing, four must also be told: 'You can't vote', and should sit down. Explain that those left standing would have been the only men who, in 1901, could vote in general elections. Ask the pupils how they feel about being told: 'You can't vote'. Discuss whether these voting arrangements were fair.

Development

Green task: Working in pairs, pupils draw up a list of what surprises them about **source a** (page 10, *History in Progress – Book 3*). To help start them off ask if they have ever seen anyone arrested, whether in reality or on TV. Encourage them to compare that with what they can see in the photograph. Aim for a class list of questions and particularly praise those that ask about the role of the photographer.

Blue task: There are three parts to this task. To begin, pupils are asked to evaluate the credibility of the individuals providing evidence (**sources b** and **c**, page 11). Encourage pupils to consider motives. This could be done as a whole class exercise. Pupils are then asked to study **sources d** and **e**, draw conclusions and cross-reference between them before answering the question (**Worksheet 1.1a**). The third part of this task could form the basis of a class discussion.

Orange task: This task gives pupils the opportunity to empathise with the suffragettes and/or someone whose property suffered at their hands. This could be scripted and acted out in front of the class, or recorded.

Plenary

Ask pupils to decide whether they believe suffragettes were justified in using violence.

Cross-curricular links

Citizenship: The nature of parliamentary representation and why it is important to vote.

1 Ruling

1.1 What did the suffragettes do to get the vote?

Worksheet 1.1a Were the suffragettes right to use violence?

3 Read **source d** on page 11 of *History in Progress – Book 3*.
   What conclusions can you draw about forced feeding?

2 Look at **source e** on page 11 of *History in Progress – Book 3*.
   What conclusions can you draw from the poster?

3 Now draw two spider diagrams, showing how the conclusions you drew from **source d** link in to the conclusions you drew from the poster in **source e**.

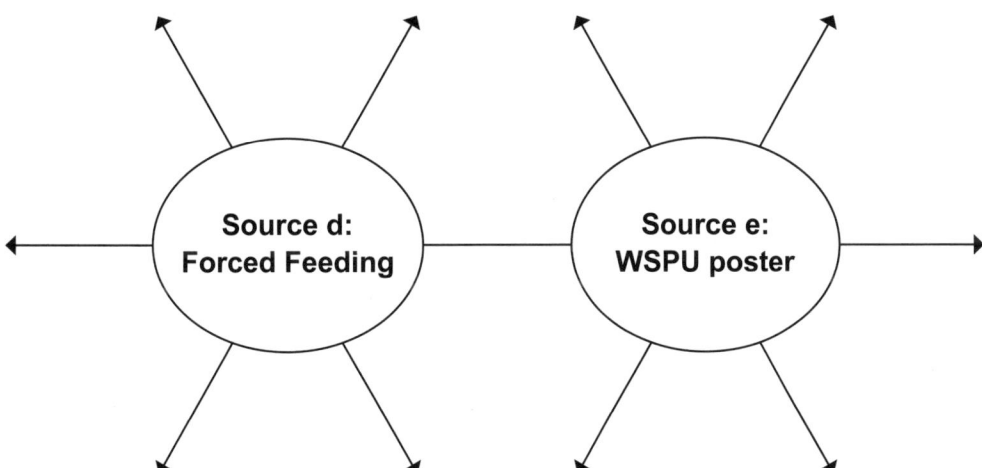

© Pearson Education Ltd 2009: History in Progress – Planning and Resource Pack 3

1 Ruling

1.1 What did the suffragettes do to get the vote?

1.1b Emily Davison: suicide or accident?

Learning objectives
- To decide whether Emily Davison's death was suicide or accident.
- To consider the differing reactions to her death.

Historical background
In 1906, Emily Davison, a woman educated at London and Oxford universities, became a militant member of the WSPU. Her activities included stone-throwing, setting letter boxes alight and attacking a Baptist minister she mistook for Lloyd George. She was frequently imprisoned for her actions and went on hunger strike many times. She once threatened suicide as a protest against being force-fed. In 1914 she was knocked down and killed by the King's horse at the Epsom Derby after she ducked under the barriers in front of it. Was this event a suicide attempt, or simply a propaganda stunt?

Teaching Activities and Learning Outcomes

Homework

Ask pupils to research another suffragette and find out what she did in the suffragette campaign to bring about votes for women. Suffragettes that could be researched include Lydia Becker, Emmeline Pankhurst, Christabel Pankhurst, Sylvia Pankhurst, Annie Kenny, Constance Lytton, Edith New, and Mary Leigh.

Pupils will be able to

- evaluate contemporary sources
- consider the evidence to decide whether or not Emily Davison's death was suicide or an accident
- analyse how the WSPU used Emily Davison's death.

Starter

Most students will focus on the photograph and on the features they can identify. Encourage them to look beyond the obvious and draw inferences from what they can see.

Development

Green task: Working in pairs, pupils should produce a lively commentary in which they both take part. Pupils will need to jot down notes or write brief guidance for themselves as to what they are going to say, but this will work best as a 'live' commentary (spoken or recorded and played back).

Blue task: Pupils evaluate the content of **sources c** and **d** (page 13, *History in Progress – Book 3*) and reach a conclusion; they then move on to **sources e** and **f** (page 13) and reach a separate conclusion. Pupils may find the provided worksheet helpful (**Worksheet 1.1b**).

Orange task: After studying **source e**, pupils should be encouraged to consider why the suffragettes created such an imposing funeral. Emily Davison was not royalty or a civic dignitary, her fame lay only within the suffragette movement and the publicity she brought to it. Who was the funeral for?

Plenary

Class discussion and vote: Suicide or accident – what is the verdict?

Cross-curricular links

Citizenship: The role and responsibility of the individual within society

1 Ruling

1.1 What did the suffragettes do to get the vote?

Worksheet 1.1b Emily Davison: suicide or accident?

2 Read through **sources c** and **d** on page 13 of *History in Progress – Book 3*.

Did Emily Davison mean to die? Sort the evidence.

Source	Evidence for suicide	Evidence against suicide
c		
d		

Now consider the people who wrote the sources. On a scale of 1–5, where 1 is least reliable and 5 is most reliable, rank their reliability:

Source	Reliability rating	Reason
c: Police report		
d: Sylvia Pankhurst		

You now have enough evidence to answer the question: Did Emily Davison mean to die? Back up your answer with evidence.

3 Read **sources e** and **f** on page 13 of *History in Progress – Book 3*.

List the differences between the sources in the table below. Continue on a separate sheet if necessary.

	Source e	Source f
Difference 1		
Difference 2		
Difference 3		
Difference 4		

Why are the sources different? Use the table below to rank the reliability of the sources as you did above.

Source	Reliability rating	Reason
e: *The Times* newspaper		
f: Christabel Pankhurst		

You now have enough evidence to account for the differences between the two sources.

1 Ruling

1.2 How did one assassination cause a war?

1.2a Why did a war break out in the Balkans?

Learning objectives
- To find out how assassination led to war in the Balkans.
- To explain the relationship between different causes

Historical background

On 28 June 1914, the heir to the Austro-Hungarian throne, Archduke Franz Ferdinand, was assassinated by Gavrilo Princip a member of the Black Hand, which was a Serbian terrorist organisation. The assassination triggered the outbreak of war in the Balkans. In many ways this was unsurprising, the region had witnessed two wars in the past three years (the First and Second Balkans wars). The underlying causes of tension in the Balkans was growing nationalist sentiment, the relative decline of the Ottoman Empire (which had controlled the region up until the second half of the nineteenth century), the emergence of Serbia, backed by its fellow Slav-state Russia, and the attempts of the Austro-Hungarian Empire to dominate the region. The assassination was taken as an opportunity for Austria-Hungary to use force to put Serbia in its place, backed by a German government ready to go to war against Russia.

Teaching Activities and Learning Outcomes

Assessment opportunity

Exploring the relationship between causes.

Pupils will be able to

- explain the arguments for and against war
- make decisions based on information
- express their understanding of how causational factors interrelate.

Starter

Pupils study **source a** (page 14, *History in Progress – Book 3*) and explain what is happening. They should discuss the picture in pairs and come up with five sentences to describe the scene. A secondary question could be asked: how could this assassination lead to war?

Development

Green task: Pupils work in groups of three. First they read through the statements made by the key players from Austria-Hungary, Germany and Serbia. Each member of the groups should choose a country and then explain to the other members of the groups the arguments for and against that country going to war. These can be written down onto **Worksheet 1.2a**.

Blue task: Pupils remain in the same work groups. Each group member should now adopt the persona of the leader of their chosen country. They each have to make a decision about going to war or not and explain their decision to the other pupils using the information presented. Their completed **Worksheet 1.2a** will help them prepare their ideas.

Orange task: The group now work together to explain three reasons why war broke out. The important element of this exercise is for the pupils to explain how the decision to go to war by one leader, had an impact on the decision making of another.

Plenary

Selected groups choose a leader to report back to the class and explain how the causes of war are related.

Cross-curricular links

Citizenship: The issue of war and decision making in government.

1 Ruling

1.2 How did one assassination cause a war?

Worksheet 1.2a Why did a war break out in the Balkans?

My chosen country..

Name of leader..

What are the arguments in favour of war?	
What are the arguments against war?	
Should my country go to war or not?	
What are the reasons for my decision?	
Why did war break out between Serbia and Austria-Hungary?	

> 1 Ruling

1.2 How did one assassination cause a war?

1.2b How did a world war begin?

Learning objectives
- To find out about the causes of the First World War.
- To use information from different sources to explain why war spread.

Historical background

The Austrian ultimatum to Belgrade was issued on 23 July 1914. It triggered a series of events which led to a European and then a world war. The following day Russia resolved to protect Serbia's interests. British attempts to summon a conference to discuss the crisis were rebuffed by Austria-Hungary and Germany although they were supported by France. Despite Serbia accepting all bar one of the points in Austria's ultimatum, it was not enough. On 28 July 1914, Austria declared war on Serbia. This triggered a series of general mobilisations: Russia followed by Austria, France (in support of Russia) and Germany. The Germans planned to attack France through Belgium. On 3 August, German troops crossed the Belgian border, triggering British entry into the war. The Balkans war had become a world war.

Teaching Activities and Learning Outcomes

Assessment Opportunity

Chronological understanding and analysing historians' interpretations through a range of media.

Pupils will be able to

- make judgements about the relative strength of the alliances and the causes of war
- draw up a timeline of events in the run up to the outbreak of war
- consider the interpretation which places the blame on Germany for the outbreak of war.

Starter

Set up a scenario of two rival groups of three pupils. Ask the class: 'what would happen if pupil X from one group was rude to pupil Y from the other?' The idea behind this exercise is for all the pupils to have a clear grasp of the escalation of the situation. The pupils' attention should then be drawn to **source a** on page 16 of *History in Progress – Book 3*. Ask them to work in pairs to explain what is being shown.

Development

Green task: Working in pairs, pupils make a judgement about the relative strength of the alliances. The exercise involves discussion before coming to a final decision. Once a pair has made their judgement, they might compare their scores with another pair. **Worksheet 1.2b** may help them.

Blue task: Using information from the previous lesson, pupils read through the events before placing them in chronological order. They should then be encouraged to identify the different phases in the outbreak of war.

Orange task: The pupils are asked to draw together their understanding of the causes of war. They might discuss their ideas first before writing them down.

Plenary

Class discussion and vote: Is Germany to blame? Vote with your feet.

1 Ruling

1.2 How did one assassination cause a war?

Worksheet 1.2b How did a world war begin?

1 Fill in the table with your scores about each country. Use the following scoring system:

5 Very strong indeed
4 Strong
3 Quite strong
2 Not so strong
1 Weak

Country	Soldiers in 1914	Money spent on military 1913-4	Battleships	Population	Overall score
Germany					
Austria-Hungary					
Italy					
Ottoman Empire					
Total scores for the Triple Alliance					
France					
Great Britain					
Russia					
Serbia					
Total scores for the Triple Entente					

Which country looks the strongest?

Which side looks stronger in 1914, the Triple Alliance or the Triple Entente?

1 Ruling

1.3 How was the First World War fought?

1.3a We want to volunteer!

Learning objectives
- To find out why people in Britain volunteered to go to war.
- To explain the impact of the outbreak of war.

Historical background
The outbreak of war in 1914 was greeted by a wave of patriotic sentiment. The British Army was relatively small in number, as was the nursing corps. The government embarked on a recruitment programme which included Lord Kitchener's famous poster appeal. Many, but not all, were swept along by war fever. Hundreds of thousands of people volunteered to serve, many out of a sense of patriotism and duty, some motivated by boredom and a sense of adventure, and others simply joined up because their friends did. A few objected to the war, fearing a bloodbath.

Teaching Activities and Learning Outcomes

Assessment opportunity

Understanding of causation and significance of events. For homework, pupils could be asked to research a current war and express their views on it.

Pupils will be able to

- assess and compare propaganda posters
- explain the reasons why people volunteered to serve in 1914
- describe the significance of the outbreak of war.

Starter

Gimme 5! The pupils' attention should be drawn to **source a** on page 18 of *History in Progress – Book 3*. What can they see? They should be asked to react to the picture with five points. A secondary question might be asked: what does this picture tell us about attitudes towards war in 1914?

Development

Green task: Task 1: Pupils create a persona by choosing a name and occupation from the supplied list. They are then to answer **task 2** and **3**, either working in a pair or on paper.

Blue task: Pupils should read through the sources on pages 18–19 of *History in Progress - Book 3*, before composing a letter explaining why they have volunteered to go to war. Pupils should be encouraged to reflect in their letter on the different reasons why others have volunteered as well as why other people have not.

Orange task: The aim of this task is to act as a conclusion to the lesson. The pupils are being asked to explain the public reaction to the outbreak of war and, therefore, its significance.

Plenary

Explaining that societal attitudes were different in 1914, hold a whole class vote: who in the class would have volunteered to serve in 1914?

Cross-curricular links

Citizenship: Issues relating to war; pacifism, patriotism and the duties of citizens.

1 Ruling

1.3 How was the First World War fought?

1.3b What was life like on the front line?

Learning objectives
- To discover what life was like on the front line.
- To evaluate how useful diaries are to historians.

Historical background
None of the volunteers in the late summer of 1914 could have foreseen the horrors of trench warfare. The last four months of 1914 were characterised by a war of movement which saw most of the British Expeditionary Force wiped out. However, the German advance on Paris was halted at the Marne and was followed by a race to the sea. Both sides then dug defensive positions and trench warfare was born. This form of warfare favoured the defender, and the German armies on the Western Front generally occupied the better positions. For the next four years, both sides were locked in a war of attrition in which millions died.

Teaching Activities and Learning Outcomes

Assessment Opportunities

Interpretation and evaluation of diaries

Pupils will be able to

- use diaries as sources of information
- weigh and question the evidence
- interpret and evaluate the use of diaries to the historian.

Starter

Quick fire questions. Why do people keep diaries? Who in the class keeps a diary and what kinds of things do they write in it? What are the strengths and weaknesses of **source a** (page 20, *History in Progress – Book 3*), for the historian researching life on the Western Front?

Development

Green task: Working in pairs, the pupils are to read the diary extracts. One pupil should read **sources b** and **c** and the other **sources d** and **e** (page 21 of *History in Progress – Book 3*), extracting three pieces of information from each source. They can then share these points firstly with each other and then with another pair of pupils in the class (**Worksheet 1.3b**).

Blue task: Pupils read through all of the sources on pages 20–21 of *History in Progress – Book 3* and then formulate questions to help evaluate diaries as evidence. The questions are based on the content of the sources and the situation and purpose of the author. The pupils can use **Worksheet 1.3b** to write down their questions. They should compare their questions with those of another pupil.

Orange task: Pupils are to use the questions formulated in **task 2** to weigh up the strengths and weaknesses of diaries. They may need help structuring their responses; they could answer the question in a chart or in paragraphs.

Plenary

The class should engage in a plenary discussion based on how useful diaries are to the historian.

> 1 Ruling

1.3 How was the First World War fought?

Worksheet 1.3b What was life like on the front line?

1 Read **sources b–e** on page 21 of *History in Progress – Book 3*. Write down three points of information from each source.

Source	Points of information
b	
b	
d	
e	

2 Evaluate **sources a–e** on pages 20–21 of *History in Progress – Book 3* by compiling a list of six questions you need to ask of them. You need two questions for each category. One example has been done already.

Category	Questions
1: Content	1 What do the diaries fail to mention? 2
2: Situation of author	3 4
3: Purpose of author	5 6

1 Ruling

1.3 How was the First World War fought?

1.3c What happened on the first day of the Battle of the Somme?

Learning objectives
- To discover what happened on 1 July 1916.
- To explain how and why interpretations differ.

Historical background
The story of the First World War is littered with tragedy from Verdun to Gallipoli. There is no story, however, which matches the pathos of the first day of the Battle of the Somme. In 1916, the German and French armies were locked in a battle for survival at Verdun. The British armies, led by Haig, were called upon by their allies to launch a diversionary offensive. They were to attack the Germans at the point where British and French armies met on the Somme. The offensive was preceded by a seven day artillery bombardment. On the morning of the battle, whistles were blown and the British soldiers emerged from the trenches and walked into No Man's Land. The Germans were waiting for them. By the end of the day there were nearly 60,000 British casualties.

Teaching Activities and Learning Outcomes

Assessment opportunity

Analysing how and why the past has been interpreted and represented in different ways.

Pupils will be able to
- categorise sources of evidence
- explain the extent to which the sources agree and differ
- explain why sources differ.

Starter

Ask the class to read **source a** (page 22, *History in Progress – Book 3*). Each pupil should come up with five points from the source. Extend this by asking if the pupils trust the source, and to explain their answer.

Development

Green task: Working in pairs or in a small group, pupils read through **sources a–f** (pages 22–23, *History in Progress – Book 3*). Using **Worksheet 1.3c (1)** or their exercise books, they sort the sources into three categories: those sources which agree that the first day on the Somme was a success, those which suggest that it was a disaster and those which suggest a mixture of the two.

Blue task: Still working in pairs, pupils try to find five similarities and differences between **sources a–f**. They record their findings in five sentences using **Worksheet 1.3c (1)**, or their exercise books.

Orange task: Pupils now discuss why the sources agree or differ. They have been given prompts to consider the context in which the sources are written, the situation and purpose of the author and the nature of the evidence. They should try and write down as many points as they can on the provided spider diagram [**Worksheet 1.3c (2)**], or in their books.

Plenary

Ask the class to provide five reasons why evidence differs.

Cross-curricular links

Citizenship: Relationship between media and war.

English: Exploring different modes of writing.

> 1 Ruling

1.3 How was the First World War fought?

Worksheet 1.3c (1) What happened on the first day of the Battle of the Somme?

1 Use the Venn diagram below to help you sort **sources a–f** (pages 22–23 of *History in Progress – Book 3*).

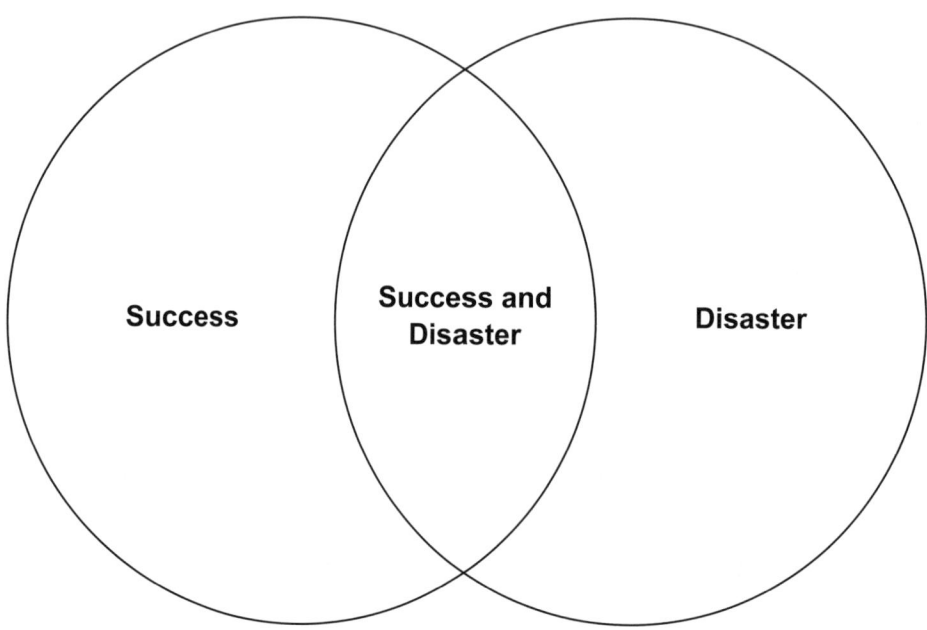

2 Write down five sentences of similarities and differences between the sources. One example has been done already.

Example

- **Source a** agrees with **source f** that German prisoners were captured on 1 July; **source a** states that "Many hundreds of enemy are prisoners in our hands", **source f** says "A good number of prisoners have been brought in on our sector".

1.

2.

3.

4.

5.

1.3 How was the First World War fought?

Worksheet 1.3c (2) What happened on the first day of the Battle of the Somme?

3 Use the spider diagram below to explain why **sources a–f** (pages 22–23 of *History in Progress – Book 3*), differ.

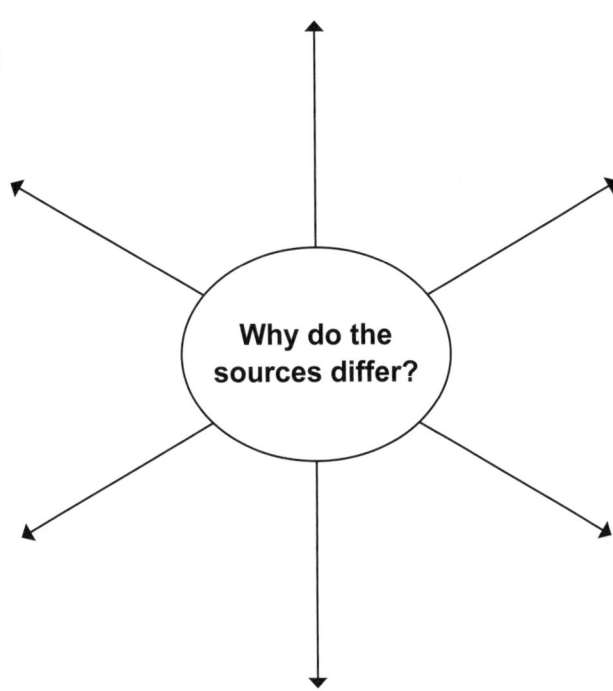

1 Ruling

1.3 How was the First World War fought?

1.3d Why were soldiers shot at dawn?

Learning objectives
- To find out about soldiers executed by their own side.
- To investigate a historical issue.

Historical background
A total of 346 British and Commonwealth soldiers were executed by their own side during the First World War. Many of those executed were suffering from shell shock or were simply caught up in the confusion of battle. The rulebook was clear and a number of offences including desertion and falling asleep whilst on duty were punishable by death. The families of those executed were to carry the shame for the next eighty or so years. Throughout that time they campaigned to clear the names of those executed. It was, and still is, an emotive issue. In 2006, the government issued a general pardon for those executed but did not consider individual pardons.

Teaching Activities and Learning Outcomes

Homework

Pupils research other soldiers 'shot at dawn' using the internet and evaluate the cases of those soldiers identified. Go to www.heinemann.co.uk/hotlinks for a good starting point.

Pupils will be able to
- undertake an enquiry
- weigh the evidence to decide whether or not individual soldiers should have been executed
- consider the issue of a pardon.

Starter

Read **source a** (page 24, *History in Progress – Book 3*) to the class. Challenge the class with the question: should the British army shoot its own soldiers?

Development

Green task: Working in pairs, the pupils should be encouraged to think of themselves as history detectives. First they should read through **source b** and **c** (page 24, *History in Progress – Book 3*). Then pupils draw up questions to ask about each case study (pages 25–26).

Blue task: Pupils reconsider each case, using their questions to decide whether or not the individual soldier in question should be pardoned or executed.

Orange task: Building on the discussion already taking place, pupils now deal with the wider issue of whether the government should reconsider individual cases, or if it was right to issue a general pardon.

Plenary

Back to the start: pupils refer back to their character from Lesson 1.3a and pass judgement on the executions.

Cross-curricular links

Citizenship: Should a government pardon those convicted nearly 100 years beforehand?

ICT opportunities

Internet research: Evaluating the cases of individual soldiers using the BBC website as a starting point.

1 Ruling

1.3 How was the First World War fought?

Taking it further!: 1.3e Remembering the War

Learning objectives
- To investigate an individual or individuals in the Great War.

Historical background
After the First World War memorials to the dead were built across the world. The Commonwealth War Graves Commission was set up to record and look after the burial places of those who had died. Ever since 1918, families and tourists have visited the battlefields and graveyards of the First World War. Although the First World War generation has now died out, there is still much memorabilia in family homes, libraries and museums. The War Graves Commission's archives are now easily accessed on the internet. The enquiry asks the pupils to undertake research within the family but it is worth pointing out that it does not have to be their family. It is also worth pointing out that we are not just looking to research about soldiers.

Teaching Activities and Learning Outcomes

Homework
Using class time, and for homework, undertake a historical enquiry

Pupils will be able to
- research family history where possible
- use the Internet and local library to undertake research
- understand how an enquiry is undertaken.

Starter
Think of five ways in which we can find out about people who served in the First World War

Development
Following the guidance on page 27 of *History in Progress – Book 3*, pupils undertake historical research. Set the investigation up just before a holiday so that pupils have time to undertake research within a family or local library over the period of a week or so.

You might like to give some lesson time to allow the pupils to use the internet for research. Set a deadline for the pupils to present their information. Encourage pupils to write up their investigations in two parts:

- Information about someone who lived at the time of the First World War.
- Reflection on the process of enquiry: what questions did they ask, who did they ask, where did they visit, how successful or unsuccessful were they and why?

The pupils have been advised in the book to photograph or photocopy valuable artefacts or original documents.

Plenary
Encourage pupils to present their findings (e.g. using PowerPoint, or creating a display of their work).

Cross-curricular links
Citizenship: Family history and remembrance.

ICT opportunities
Researching on the internet: a good starting point is the Commonwealth War Graves site. A link can be found at www.heinemann.co.uk/hotlinks. Pupils could use PowerPoint to present their findings.

> 1 Ruling

1.4 What was the impact of the end of the First World War?

1.4a A land fit for heroes?

Learning objectives
- To find out what life was like in Britain after the First World War.
- To analyse change and continuity.

Historical background
The end of the First World War brought huge challenges for Britain. Over 600,000 of her soldiers had been killed in four years of war and another 1.6 million had been wounded. The expense of the war exceeded £8,000 million. The British government led by David Lloyd George also faced problems across the Empire, from India and Palestine to Ireland. The considerable sacrifice of war led to raised expectations of meaningful social reform. These expectations were fanned by Lloyd George who promised in November 1918, that he would make 'Britain a fit country for heroes to live in'. This was easier said than done; over the coming years some social housing was built with government subsidies but unemployment remained high as industry struggled to readjust to peacetime conditions.

Teaching Activities and Learning Outcomes

Assessment opportunity

Understanding the extent of change.

Pupils will be able to

- show empathy for those returning from war service
- assess the extent of change post 1918
- explain the reactions of servicemen to post war conditions.

Starter

Gimme five: What five things that those returning from service abroad would hope for most? Make a list and compare with a work partner. How many are the same?

Development

Green task: Pupils use the character they chose from Lesson 1.3a and form groups of four or six. Using the list begun in the starter activity, they draw up a list of demands for change. When completed and approved, they should compare their list to that of another group.

Blue task: Staying in their groups, pupils read the experiences of the ex-servicemen. They then answer the questions, either in groups or individually in writing.

Orange task: Back into character, each pupil writes a speech explaining their war record, expectations, and the extent of change which has taken place as well as a judgement on Lloyd George's record.

Plenary

Some of the pupils undertaking the orange task could read their speeches out. If there is time, the class could vote as to whether the soldiers' expectations have been met.

Cross-curricular links

Citizenship: The role of government and the Welfare State.

1 Ruling

1.4 What was the impact of the end of the First World War?

1.4b What was the reaction in Germany to the end of the war?

Learning objectives
- To find out the reaction to the end of the war in Germany.
- To reach a judgement about the significance of defeat.

Historical background
The end of the war came as a shock to most Germans. The collapse on the Home Front was mirrored in military defeat on the Western Front. At the end of September, General Ludendorff suggested to the German government that they seek an armistice. Negotiations which followed with the allies were based on the assumption of the German government that an armistice would be based on President Wilson's fourteen points. At the start of November, mutiny broke out and the Kaiser was forced to abdicate. Hostilities ceased on 11 November 1918. Many in Germany refused to accept that Germany had been defeated and expected that Germany would avoid a punitive settlement. The Treaty of Versailles of 1919 was a bitter humiliation, especially the war guilt clause, the demand for reparations, the destruction of Germany's military might and loss of territories. Communist revolution in Germany was put down by an alliance of army, state and Freikorps. In 1919, the myth emerged that Germany had been 'stabbed in the back'. Defeat and its aftermath seriously undermined Germany stability.

Teaching Activities and Learning Outcomes

Homework
Ask pupils to research the main points of the Treaty of Versailles.

Assessment Opportunity
Understanding significance of events.

Pupils will be able to
- investigate evidence
- empathise with a German soldier at the end of the war
- discuss the significance of certain aspects of the defeat.

Starter
Pupils should be directed to look at **sources a** and **b** (page 30, *History in Progress – Book 3*). Ask them to provide two or three comments which surprise them.

Development
Green task: Pupils could work in pairs to sift through the items in the suitcase (**Worksheet 1.4b**).

Blue task: Pupils use the information from the green task to empathise with German soldiers reacting to defeat. Encourage pupils to consider the possible range of reactions from shock to anger.

Orange task: Working in pairs, pupils discuss the different aspects of defeat (e.g. refusal to accept defeat, anger against politicians, expectations of a just peace, humiliation of Versailles, reparations, loss of land, communist revolution, 'stab in the back', political polarisation). They then explain the significance of four of them. **Worksheet 1.4b** will help them clarify their ideas.

Plenary
Class discussion: What was the significance for Germany of defeat in 1918?

1 Ruling

1.4 What was the impact of the end of the First World War?

Worksheet 1.4b What was the reaction in Germany to the end of the war?

Study the evidence in the suitcase (**sources a–g**, pages 30–31 of *History in Progress – Book 3*). For each piece of evidence explain what it tells you about the impact of the end of the war.

Evidence	What it tells us about the impact of the end of the war
Source a	
Source b	
Source c	
Source d	
Source e	
Source f	
Source g	
Letter	

Now choose four aspects which made the defeat so significant for Germany. Write down the source(s) from which you got your information and explain the significance of each one in the table below. One example has been completed for you.

Aspect	Sources	Significance
Reduced armed forces	f, g	The Treaty of Versailles led to the destruction of Germany's armed forces. Germany was not allowed an airforce and her tanks were broken up. This was significant because Germany was powerless to resist the Allies and was humiliated.

1 Ruling

1.4 What was the impact of the end of the First World War?

1.4c How was the League of Nations perceived?

Learning objectives
- To examine the founding and actions of the League of Nations.
- To assess the meanings in contemporary cartoons.

Historical background
The Treaty of Versailles led to the creation of the League of Nations. The aims of the League were to make the world a better place and to keep the peace. Despite these lofty aims, the League was weakened from the start. Despite being the brainchild of American President Woodrow Wilson, an isolationist Congress barred the USA from joining. Germany and the Soviet Union were also initially not involved in the League. The League operated on the basis of collective security which, in reality, meant that it relied heavily on Britain and France because it did not have an army of its own. That said, the League successfully resolved a number of disputes in the 1920s. An important turning point in the history of the League was the Wall Street Crash in 1929 and the Great Depression. Thereafter, all states including Britain and France were less willing to support the League. In the 1930s, countries such as Japan and Italy aggressively challenged the peace; the League was relatively powerless to stop them doing so.

Teaching Activities and Learning Outcomes

Assessment opportunity

Evaluation of evidence

Pupils will be able to

- interpret cartoons
- show how interpretations change over time
- evaluate the use of cartoons.

Starter

Working in pairs, pupils list the images in **source a** (page 32, *History in Progress – Book 3*) and give suggestions as to what those images mean. Each pair shares their list with another pair.

Development

Green task: Working in pairs, pupils interpret **sources b–d** (page 33, *History in Progress – Book 3*) as they did with **source a**.

Blue task: Pupils should use the text on pages 32–33, as well as **sources a–d**, to explain five ways in which Low's attitude towards the League changes. They then move on to explaining why it changed.

Orange task: Pupils evaluate Low's cartoons by considering the content, context, situation and purpose of the author. They have been given two statements to discuss to provoke them to consider whether or not Low's cartoons are useful to the historian The task can be completed orally or on paper.

Plenary

Class discussion: Are David Low's cartoons important and why?

Cross-curricular links

Citizenship: The United Nations, Collective Security and how to keep the peace.

> 1 Ruling

1.4 What was the impact of the end of the First World War?

1.4d Was appeasement the right policy?

Learning objectives
- To find out why Britain adopted a policy of appeasement.
- To investigate a historical problem.

Historical background
Hitler's foreign policy objectives included the destruction of the Treaty of Versailles. For a majority of Germans the Treaty was a national humiliation which needed to be reversed. In 1933, Germany left the League of Nations and by the mid 1930s the League was much weakened. From 1935 onwards, the Nazi regime in Germany slowly but surely undermined the Treaty; conscription, the Rhineland, Anschluss and the Czech crisis revised the Treaty. Many in Britain and France were prepared to accept such revision of the Treaty as a prize worth paying for secured peace. Britain's priorities at the beginning of the 1930s were the protection of its Empire, social improvement and economic recovery. However, from the mid 1930s it recognised that Nazi Germany was an increasing threat and started rearming. In September 1938, Neville Chamberlain became Prime Minister. He followed a policy of appeasement in response to German demands on the Sudetenland.

Teaching Activities and Learning Outcomes

Assessment Opportunity

Investigating a historical problem.

Pupils will be able to

- explain the issues related to the policy of appeasement in the 1930s
- explore the alternatives facing Chamberlain in the late 1930s
- make a decision as to the pros and cons of appeasement.

Starter

The aim of the starter is to confront pupils with a threatening situation and provoke a class discussion. What do they do: take the bully on, persuade other pupils to join in, or attempt to appease the bully?

Development

Green task: Ask pupils to give five reasons why the Germans wished to revise the Versailles treaty. Some of their ideas might come from Lesson 1.4b. **Task 2** provokes pupils to think more carefully about why the Allies did not react to German revision of the Treaty in the 1930s. They might refer to the impact of the Great Depression, different attitudes and priorities in Britain and France, or the desire for peace.

Blue task: In groups, pupils discuss the options presented. Each group should choose a representative to feed back to the rest of the class.

Orange task: Encourage pupils to consider their view on appeasement. They could write a summary arguing one way or the other (appeasement was a mistake or was a reasonable policy given the circumstances). This summary might be written as a speech to be delivered as part of a class debate.

Plenary

For those classes which have completed the blue task, hold a vote on Chamberlain's most appropriate course of action. If pupils have worked on the orange task (or have completed speeches for / against appeasement), hold a debate on the pros and cons of appeasement, ending with a class vote.

Cross-curricular links

PSHE: Exploring bullying and how to best deal with the threat posed by bullies.

1.5 What were the key moments of the Second World War?

1.5a Dunkirk: victory or defeat?

Learning objectives
- To find out about Dunkirk in 1940.
- To discover that one event can be interpreted in different ways.

Historical background

The German invasion of France in May 1940, caught the French, Belgian and British armies by surprise. By the end of the month they were all staring defeat in the face. The British army fell back to the Channel and the beaches near Dunkirk. The German panzer divisions chasing the British were certain of victory and paused to refuel and rest before the planned campaign to capture Paris. As British and French troops assembled on the beaches, the call went out for ships of all sizes to go to France and rescue the Allied troops. 340,000 men were rescued, although their equipment was left behind. It was a crushing defeat but it made it possible for Britain to continue in the war. The myth of Dunkirk was born.

Teaching Activities and Learning Outcomes

Assessment opportunity

Explaining how and why different interpretations of the past have arisen or been constructed

Pupils will be able to

- interpret information from sources
- explain how and why interpretations differ.

Starter

Gimme five: What five words would you use to describe the message of **source a** (page 36, *History in Progress – Book 3*). Encourage pupils to share their five words with each other.

Development

Green task: Pupils can work on their own to read through the sources, summarising each in a written sentence. Alternatively they can work in pairs with one pupil summarising **sources b–d** (pages 36–37), *History in Progress – Book 3*), and the other **sources e–g** (also pages 36–37).

Blue task: In pairs or groups, pupils are asked to come up with the five reasons why the sources differ. They can be helped come to their conclusions by considering the situation and purpose of the author and the nature of the evidence. Pupils might present their points on a spider diagram.

Orange task: Pupils should show their understanding of why and how interpretations differ by writing a speech to be made by their chosen character. In their speech they should explain the events of Dunkirk, tailoring their points to the audience. The speeches can be read out in groups or in class.

Plenary

The plenary is based on the blue task: so why do interpretations differ? There could be a class discussion which pulls together all of the points made.

> 1 Ruling

1.5 What were the key moments of the Second World War?

1.5b Pearl Harbour: what is the story?

Learning objectives
- To find out why the USA joined the Second World War.
- To tell the story of Pearl Harbour.

Historical background
The outbreak of war in Europe meant that only the United States of America of the Great Powers had sufficient military forces to prevent Japanese domination of South East Asia. The fall of France in 1940 led to Japanese occupation of parts of Indo-China. By late 1941, the Imperial Japanese government led by General Hideki Tojo had come to the conclusion that dominance in South East Asia was conditional on the destruction of the American fleet based at Pearl Harbour in Hawaii. To dominate the region, Japan had to dominate the seas. Tension between the United States of America and Japan increased through the autumn until, on 7 December, the Japanese attacked. The following day the United States of America declared war on Japan. On 11 December Germany declared war on the United States of America.

Teaching Activities and Learning Outcomes

Assessment opportunity

Selecting, organising and using relevant information.

Pupils will be able to

- organise information into chronological sequence
- make judgements about a historical event
- speculate as to why decisions were made.

Starter

Set the scene of 1940 by reading Churchill's speech (**source a**, page 38, *History in Progress – Book 3*). In whole class discussion, tease out Britain's predicament (the country was alone) and potential salvation (the USA joining the war).

Development

Green task: Pupils draw up a timeline of events using the information presented.

Blue task: In groups, pupils discuss the four statements and consider the issue of Churchill's possible role. Each group should choose a spokesperson who will report back to the class.

Orange task: Still in groups, ask pupils to come up with sub-questions which will help them answer the overall question about whether the Americans did or didn't know about Pearl Harbour in advance.

Plenary

Vote with your feet: It doesn't matter whether the pupils have completed the orange task or not. Ask pupils to position themselves in the room according to whether they believe that the Americans knew in advance about the attack or not.

1 Ruling

1.5 What were the key moments of the Second World War?

1.5c What was the significance of Stalingrad?

Learning objectives
- To find out about the battle of Stalingrad.
- To explain the significance of an event.

Historical background

On 22 June 1941, the Axis powers invaded the Soviet Union in Operation Barbarossa. Initially they swept all before them capturing millions of prisoners and advancing across thousands of miles of territory. In October 1941, the German army was within sight of Moscow but was halted by the winter weather. The following spring, Hitler ordered his armies south. The Sixth Army was instructed to capture the strategically important city of Stalingrad. From August 1942 to February 1943, one of the most significant battles of the war was fought; the Soviets came out victorious. The following spring the German armies launched a successful campaign at Kharkov, only to be pushed back by the Soviet summer offensive of 1943, which included the tank battle at Kursk.

Teaching Activities and Learning Outcomes

Assessment opportunity

Explaining the significance of an event

Pupils will be able to

- explain similarities and differences between sources
- use sources to test a hypothesis
- use sources to explain the significance of event.

Starter

Source a (page 40, *History in Progress – Book 3*) is read out to the class. Quickfire questions: what are the main points made in **source a**? What other turning points can they think of?

Development

Green task: Encourage pupils to read the text (page 40, *History in Progress – Book 3*) which provides a context to the sourcework. Pupils then study **sources b** and **c** (pages 40–41), and identify the differences. This could be done using a spider diagram (**Worksheet 1.5c**). They should give reasons for why the sources differ.

Blue task: The pupils work in pairs to agree which sources fully agree with the hypothesis in **source a**, which partly agree and which disagree (**Worksheet 1.5c**).

Orange task: Using the '5Ws', pupils evaluate each source and come to a judgement about whether they trust each of them sufficiently to use them. The evaluation should be discussed with a work partner. The summary assignment might be set as a homework task. Pupils will need to be given some guidance about how to structure the task using the sources which they have identified as being useful.

Plenary

Which of the sources is most useful to the historian investigating the significance of Stalingrad?

1 Ruling

1.5 What were the key moments of the Second World War?

Worksheet 1.5c What was the significance of Stalingrad?

1 Use the spider diagram below to generate three differences between the views of the authors of **sources b** and **c** (pages 40–41, *History in Progress – Book 3*). Give two reasons why the sources might differ.

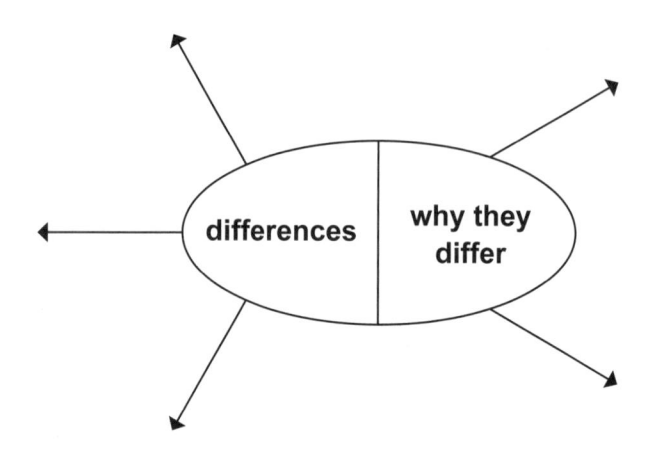

2 After reading **sources b–f** (also pages 40–41), fill in the following table writing down which sources fully support the hypothesis, which partly support it and which disagree.

	Fully support	Partly support	Disagree
Sources			

3 Evaluate the provenance of each source and then come to a decision about whether you can trust it enough to use in support of your final answer. Remember to ask the 5Ws (page 186, *History in Progress – Book 3*) of each source.

Source	Evaluation	Trust: Yes, no, maybe
b		
c		
d		
e		
f		
g		

1.5 What were the key moments of the Second World War?

1.5d Questions for Martha

Learning objectives
- To learn about D-Day through the eyes of one person.
- To evaluate the usefulness of the evidence.

Historical background
On 6 June 1944, the Allies launched the opening of the Western Front in Europe: D-Day. Thousands of ships crossed the English Channel to land troops in Normandy. Some managed to get ashore with few problems but others, notably the Americans landing at Omaha Beach, met fierce resistance. Following the troops were medical staff on hospital ships, keen to help out in any way they could.

Teaching Activities and Learning Outcomes

Assessment opportunity

Evaluating evidence.

Pupils will be able to
- interpret evidence
- ask further questions
- evaluate the use of Martha's evidence.

Starter

Class discussion: Why is one person's eyewitness story useful?

Development

Green task: The pupils will need to read through **source a** (page 43, *History in Progress – Book 3*). They can do this in pairs or as a class. Once the source has been read, pupils should work in pairs to list at least ten points about D-Day from the story.

Blue task: Pupils need to now become more critical of the evidence. Working in pairs, pupils should draw up a list of six questions to ask about D-Day to get a broader picture. Pairs of pupils should share their questions with other pairs.

Orange task: Pupils evaluate the usefulness of source a to those historians investigating D-Day. The evaluation task can be completed orally or on paper.

Plenary

Class discussion: On balance, is **source a** useful or not?

> 1 Ruling

1.5 What were the key moments of the Second World War?

1.5d Hiroshima: use of the bomb, right or wrong?

Learning objectives
- To learn about the use of the atom bomb on Hiroshima in August 1945.
- To debate the arguments for and against the use of the bomb.

Historical background
By 1945, Japan had been beaten by the superior military might of the USA and her allies. However, the Japanese continued to put up fierce resistance as American troops stormed strategically important islands including Iwo Jima and Okinawa. In May 1945, the American air force launched a huge offensive aimed at the Japanese mainland. It shattered Japanese industry and her ability to continue fighting the war. However, despite the destruction of Japanese towns and cities, including the capital Tokyo, the Japanese government did not surrender. In 1942, the Allies set up the Manhattan Project to make a nuclear weapon capable of destruction on an unforeseen scale. By August 1945, US$2 billion later, the first bomb was ready to be used. On 6 August it was dropped on Hiroshima.

Teaching Activities and Learning Outcomes

Assessment Opportunity

Investigating a historical problem with an opportunity to write up conclusions for homework.

Pupils will be able to

- ask questions about the dropping of the bomb
- identify points for and against the dropping of the bomb
- argue a case about the dropping of the bomb.

Starter

Source a (page 44, *History in Progress – Book 3*), should be read out loud. In pairs, pupils should come up with three points from the source about the impact of the bomb. Quick class vote: should the Americans have dropped the bomb?

Develpment

Green task: Pupils work in groups to come up with questions raised by the dropping of the bomb e.g. why was the bomb dropped on Hiroshima? Why on this date? Did they know how many Japanese civilians would die? The list of questions should be added to as pupils read through the sources (pages 44–45, *History in Progress – Book 3*).

Blue task: Using the information in the sources (pages 44–45), pupils identify the arguments for and against dropping the bomb. They could share their list with other pupils.

Orange task: Encourage pupils to write up an argument about the use of the bomb. They can take one of three stances. Arguments should be supported with evidence from the sources (pages 44–45) and any other evidence picked up through research.

Plenary

Class debate: Hiroshima: use of the bomb, right or wrong?

Cross-curricular links

Citizenship: At which point is the use of force acceptable and can we justify the use of atomic weapons?

1.6 How did governments respond after the Second World War?

1.6a Has the United Nations helped to create a better world?

Learning objectives
- To consider how strong and effective the United Nations has been since 1945.
- To compare and contrast a range of case studies to reach an overall judgement.

Historical background
President Roosevelt first used the title 'United Nations' (UN) at the Arcadia Conference in Washington in January 1942. The UN were the Allies who had fought the Axis Powers to establish a post-war world in which there would be 'a permanent system of general security'. In June 1945, fifty nations signed the Charter of the UN at the UN Conference on International Organisation held in San Francisco. It officially came into existence on 24 October after the Charter had been ratified. The old League of Nations officially dissolved itself on 18 April 1946.

Teaching Activities and Learning Outcomes

Assessment opportunity

Using evidence to reach and support a conclusion; evaluating UN success and refining original ideas in the light of new information.

Pupils will be able to

- suggest at least two reasons why the UN was an improvement upon the League of Nations
- use selected information to support ideas about why the UN has had some success.

Starter

Working in pairs, pupils think of three ideas that could make the world a better place and feedback to the class. Write suggestions up on the board, grouping them into categories. Pupils can name the categories and discuss which ideas they could action, and which ideas organisations would have to deal with.

Development

Green Task: Pupils use **source a** on page 46 of *History in Progress – Book 3*, to think about the cartoonist's views of the UN and the League of Nations. Ask pupils how the UN might be better equipped to help make the world a better place.

Blue Task: You could go through the first event as a class to model the type of reasoning and judgement required. Pupils then evaluate the other events and compare grades with a partner. Encourage pupils to discuss any differences of opinion and to explain why they think the UN deserves a particular grade.

Orange Task: Pupils should use the information they have read, and the causes for success or failure they have discussed, in their answer to this question. Pupils could use each bullet point to form a paragraph in their report. **Worksheet 1.6a** has been provided to help with the blue and orange tasks.

Plenary

Explain who Ban Ki Moon is. Ask three pupils to say one thing they would do as Secretary General of the UN to make the world a better place. Let the class vote for the best, or most realistic idea.

Cross-curricular links

Citizenship: The role and responsibility of the individual within society, and the role of supranational organisations like the UN in world affairs.

ICT opportunities

Pupils could explore the UN website. Go to www.heinemann.co.uk/hotlinks for the link.

1 Ruling

1.6 How did governments respond after the Second World War?

Worksheet 1.6a Has the United Nations helped to create a better world?

5 Read through the UN report card on page 47 of *History in Progress – Book 3*. Use the information in the reports to give the UN a grade from A – E for achievement (where A is excellent and E is poor result), and 1–5 for effort (where 1 is excellent effort and 5 is poor effort). Once you have done this, explain your grade using details from the report card.

'Subject'	Grade	Comments: why have you awarded this grade?
1950–53: Korea		
1956–67: Egypt and the Suez Canal		
1960–64: Central Africa, the Congo		
1949–present: India-Pakistan border		
1956–68: Eastern Europe		
1945–today: the world		

Now you are ready to write the full end of term report. You might want to set out your report using the sentences below to begin each paragraph.

END OF TERM REPORT: THE UN

The UN has performed well in a number of areas, such as…

The reasons for these successes include…

However, it has not all been good news. The UN must improve…

Overall, the UN has….

Next term, the UN ought to try to improve in the following areas:

-

-

1 Ruling

1.6 How did governments respond after the Second World War?

1.6b Why did it take sixteen years for Britain to join the European Community?

Learning objectives
- To explore the reasons for and against British membership of the European Community.
- To make judgements about who was to blame for the delay in British membership.

Historical background
In 1957, Belgium, France, Germany, Holland, Italy and Luxemburg (the Six) signed the Treaty of Rome to form the European Community (EC), an organisation designed to integrate their economies. It was hoped that tying European economies and governments closely together would make another war impossible. Harold Macmillan (British Prime Minister from 1957–63) was a strong Europhile, but thought entry into the EC politically unviable. He retired in 1963, largely due to ill health and the Profumo scandal.

Teaching Activities and Learning Outcomes

Assessment opportunity

Evaluating and supporting their choice of the most important considerations for joining the EC; judging Macmillan's responsibility for failure.

Pupils will be able to

- decide which arguments concerning membership of the EC were most important
- use these decisions to support an argument about entry into the EC
- consider how far Macmillan was to blame for the British not joining the EC 1957–63.

Starter

Write the starter question on the board and hold a class vote based on pupils' gut reaction to it. Ask pupils to explain their votes. Discuss language, culture, history, trade, geography etc. before voting again to see if views have shifted.

Development

Green task: Worksheet 1.6b (1) will help sort the arguments into whether they are important points or not. Discuss criteria for decisions and model the first two cards with them. Once pupils have discussed a card, they place it on the 'zone of decision' [**Worksheet 1.6b (2)**]. Select pupils to explain their top three cards to the class to provoke debate about the order as a mini-plenary.

Blue task: Pupils decide whether the cards they consider important are for or against EC entry and if these cards, on balance, support entry or not. This should give them starting points for **tasks 3b** and **4**.

Orange task: This could either be a written answer for homework, or used as a class debate.

Plenary

Explain that Britain is now a member of the European Union (EU), the successor to the EC, and that some people want Britain to leave the EU. Encourage pupils to think back over the original arguments for and against the EC, and hold a vote on whether Britain should leave the EU. Discuss the vote to draw out the arguments used in the tasks.

Cross-curricular links

Citizenship: The meaning of British sovereignty; is membership of supranational organisations a threat?

ICT opportunities

History in Progress – LiveText CD 3: electronic activity.

1 Ruling

1.6 How did governments respond after the Second World War?

Worksheet 1.6b (1) Why did it take sixteen years for Britain to join the European Community?

1 Read a card and working with a partner decide whether you think it is an important point to consider, or an unimportant one.

When you have made your decision, place it in the appropriate place on the 'zone of decision' diagram. This does not have to be a final decision, you can move the cards as you read other cards and decide that they are more/less important than the cards already on the diagram!

The British Public: We don't know much about Europe. We'll join the EC if it is in our best interest, but we hear such mixed messages from the government and the media.

British Farmers: The French want to use EC money to help their farmers make cheap food. If we join the EC, the common market will mean loads of cheap food coming from Europe. We'll go bust and Britain will have to rely on foreigners fro all her food.

Russia is growing stronger and stronger. If it can put satellites into space, surely it can send missiles to our door.

The New European Community will be a huge new trading area of 160million people. Can British industry afford to be left out of this common market?

Commonwealth Countries: Our livelihoods depend on trade with Britain. If Britain joins the common market, the EC will tax our exports so the British won't buy them. And don't forget our common history, our British roots.

The Cabinet: The French are jealous of our Commonwealth and want us to abandon it to join the EC. We must not join the EC until 'the Six' have changed the rules to suit our Commonwealth trade. If we say that Britain wants to join the EC too early, the French will think we are desperate and won't agree to change the rules.

Now that we have lost India and Ghana, how much life is really left in the British Empire?

If we stay out of the EC, will France or Germany dominate this new Europe in future?

The lawyers: We have one of the oldest Parliaments and legal systems in the world. If Britain joins the EC, our parliament will have to accept the laws made by the European Council of Ministers. The European Court of Justice could overrule our own courts. We will lose our hard won sovereignty.

America is not the friend we once thought. Look at the way it stopped our efforts in the Suez Crisis

Will the Commonwealth guarantee Britain's status as a world power in the years to come?

1 Ruling

1.6 How did governments respond after the Second World War?

Worksheet 1.6b (2) Why did it take sixteen years for Britain to join the European Community?

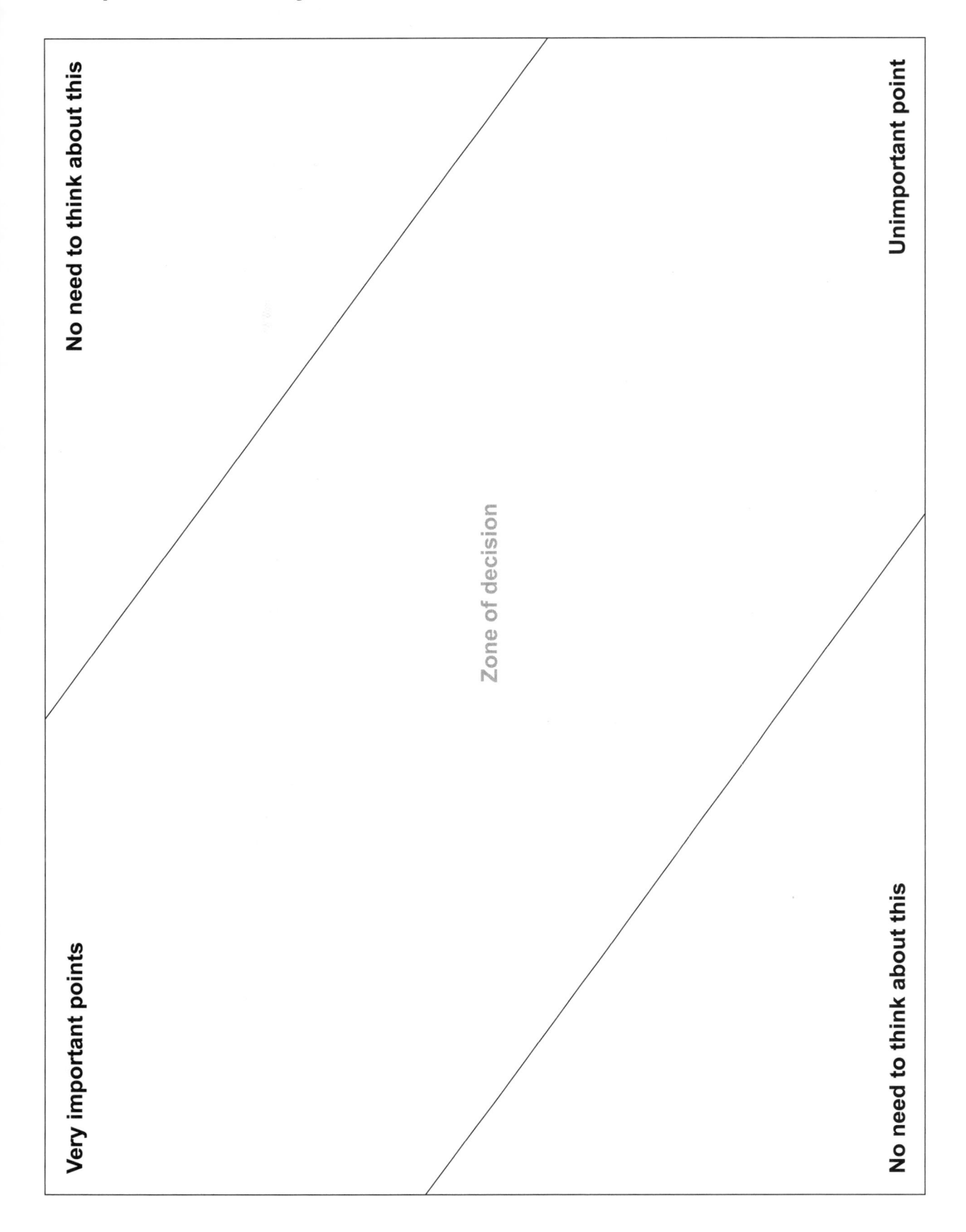

No need to think about this

Unimportant point

Zone of decision

Very important points

No need to think about this

© Pearson Education Ltd 2009: History in Progress – Planning and Resource Pack 3

> 1 Ruling

1.6 How did governments respond after the Second World War?

1.6c Devolution: what's in it for us?

Learning objectives
- To debate whether Scotland and Wales should become independent from the United Kingdom.
- To create and present an argument based on a range of evidence.

Historical background
The Scottish National Party (SNP) came to power in Scotland in 2007. They published a White Paper called Choosing Scotland's Future, the paper included complete independence as a possible option. The SNP intend to hold an independence referendum in 2010. Both Labour and the Conservatives are firmly against Scottish independence. Support for Welsh independence remains a fringe movement.

Teaching Activities and Learning Outcomes

Assessment opportunity

Building a chronological framework for understanding the debate and using new knowledge to support an argument.

Pupils will be able to

- decide whether events in the Scottish and Welsh past support modern demands for independence
- use information to make and support an argument in small groups and as a whole class.

Starter

Ask pupils about what makes them think of themselves as a particular national identity: place of birth, language, history, food, customs etc. This could also develop into a discussion on where the different nationalities overlap as well as differ and an examination of cultural events and sport.

Development

Green Task: Try to ensure an even split of the class into pairs researching Scotland and Wales.

Blue task: Pupils debate the same question three times. Appoint one pupil in each group (pair, four, eight), as secretary: their task is to write down the group's final answer, and the three most important reasons for this decision.

Orange task: If there is no natural split after the group discussions, you will have to make one group propose and the other oppose the motion. Pupils work in their groups to prepare the two speakers with arguments for their side of the motion, and for attacking the other side. You could allow the group to choose two principal speakers, or you could nominate them yourself. You could change the layout of your class to mirror the House of Commons, or with the principal speakers at the front.

Plenary

Back to the Start: Ask pupils to consider the question on page 51 of the student book. Encourage them to use arguments from this lesson and the previous two lessons on supranational organisations.

Cross-curricular links

Citizenship: The nature of national identity; the changing structure of political power within Britain.

ICT opportunities

Investigate the current arguments for and against further devolvement of power, or even independence for Scotland and Wales on the Party for Wales and the Scottish National Party websites: www.heinemann.co.uk/hotlinks

1 Ruling

1.7 Who had an impact in the struggle for civil rights in the USA?

1.7a How did Rosa Parks transform America?

Learning objectives
- To identify reasons why an individual protest became a national phenomenon.
- To reflect on the importance of events surrounding the actions of an individual.

Historical background
For much of the preceding century the civil rights of the black population of the United States were determined by the 'Jim Crow' laws. After the Second World War, black activists were emboldened by the equal sacrifices of the recent war and began to challenge those laws through targeted protests designed to highlight the condition of the black man in 'The Land of the Free.'

Teaching Activities and Learning Outcomes

Assessment opportunity

Pupils' selection of relevant information to identify reasons behind opinions and actions of civil rights activists.

Pupils will be able to

- identify the nature and purpose of the 'Jim crow' laws
- explain how opponents of the 'Jim Crow' laws were able to publicise their campaign
- develop a conclusion as to the importance of individual action in the civil rights struggle in the USA.

Starter

Working in pairs, pupils should identify common rights and freedoms and then list them in order of importance. An extension question might probe more deeply into which ones they feel they could do without, or would abolish first and why?

Development

Green task: Pupils use **sources a** and **b** (pages 52–53, *History in Progress – Book 3*) to identify the nature and extent of the 'Jim Crow' laws and their effect on the lifestyle of black Americans. Ask pupils to select one of these laws as the most restrictive / oppressive to stimulate further debate and build awareness of the impact these laws had on black ambitions and aspirations.

Blue task: **Source c** on page 53 can be analysed as part of a Nature, Origin, Purpose (NOP) exercise before discussion on whether or not such a cartoon should have been produced in order to draw attention to a cause. Using **source e** (page 54), pupils should consider whether there was a real alternative to what Rosa was doing.

Orange task: Emphasise that pupils need to take care to achieve a sense of balance. Before starting discuss the characteristics of a non-partisan article with the class.

Plenary

Ask pupils to quickly list and then vote on other different forms of protest. If the form chosen by Rosa Parks is considered too risky, what other types were likely to be effective and why?

Cross-curricular links

Citizenship: The importance of human rights

ICT opportunities

The interview can be done through 'hot seating' a student in the role of Rosa and digitally videoing the results. The report can be completed using a text editor.

> 1 Ruling

1.7 Who had an impact in the struggle for civil rights in the USA?

1.7b Why was Malcolm X assassinated?

Learning objectives
- To understand why a civil rights leader was assassinated.
- To use sources to provide evidence for the motive behind Malcolm X's murder.

Historical background
Rosa Parks was not the only civil right activist of the late 1950s and early 1960s. Throughout the 1950s, organised groups sprang up with their own ideas about what liberty should mean for black Americans. Amongst the most strident was 'The Nation of Islam' whose most vocal proponent was Malcolm X. In 1965, at the height of the civil rights protests, Malcolm X was gunned down.

Assessment opportunity
Using source material to ask relevant questions, draw inferences and make deductions.

Teaching Activities and Learning Outcomes
- finding information in the text that enables pupils to define what Malcolm X believed in
- explaining how Malcolm's change of views might affect the way that people saw and reacted to him
- solving and explaining why Malcolm X was assassinated.

Starter
As a class, ask pupils to make a short list of famous people and discuss why they are considered famous. Pupils can use a spider diagram for this. The answers can be used to probe more deeply in to the nature of fame, and the inherent problems of being famous.

Development
Green task: Pupils use the **factfile** data on page 56 of *History in Progress – Book 3* to learn about Malcolm X and what he believed in. Encourage pupils to identify the sort of people that might have supported, as well as opposed, his views.

Blue task: Pupils are encouraged to think about how each piece of evidence is enabling them to build a more complex profile of Malcolm X. Pupils should use the understanding gained in the blue task to help them consider what effect Malcolm X's change of views might have had.

Orange task: Pupils are asked to bring all the evidence together to draw conclusions about not just why the Nation of Islam was behind the assassination, but also the motives behind it. The exercise could also be completed as a debate with suggestions that white anti civil rightists could have been behind the murder.

Plenary
Pupils have studied two people who took very different routes for advancing the cause of civil rights. Ask the class to vote on who had the biggest impact. Extend this by asking: why?

Cross-curricular links
Citizenship: The role of religion in unifying and leading people.

ICT opportunities
Pupils could create a PowerPoint display about the assassination (detailing evidence for the motive and suspects).

1.7 Who had an impact in the struggle for civil rights in the USA?

1.7c Why was Martin Luther King seen as a threat?

Learning objectives
- To find out about the impact that Martin Luther King had on the civil rights movement.
- To be able to use evidence to develop and present a historical conclusion.

Historical background
In the mid 1960s, at the height of the agitation for Civil Rights, Dr. Martin Luther King provided a voice for many black citizens of the USA through which they could express their hopes and ambitions for a better future. Today his contribution to a fairer society is nationally recognised, but at the time his violent death reminded many that there were those amongst the American public who disagreed with what he said and what he stood for.

Assessment opportunity
Using source evidence to reach a judgement about a historical figure, and to evaluate his importance in relation to other leading civil rights activists.

Pupils will be able to
- describe and use additional sources to develop an interpretation of a contemporary photograph
- reach conclusions about the nature of the challenge Dr. Martin Luther King posed
- to identify and use evidence to support a conclusion.

Starter
Give students ten seconds to look at **source a** on page 58 of *History in Progress – Book 3*. Ask them to give a quick 'gut' reaction of the image by writing down some key words. Pupils share their words with a partner before jointly coming up with a headline that describes the scene. Pairs then share their headlines with the class so that pupils become aware of how interpretations of the source can differ. Pupils now think of questions, individually or as a class, about what more they need to know in order to 'understand' the incident.

Development
Green task: Individually at first and then in pairs, pupils are asked to give an initial view of what they believe is happening in **source a**. Ask the pupils to consider the circumstances under which such a picture may have been published and by whom. Teachers' may consider adding the two written sources one at a time to explore the differences in the students' impressions of the event.

Blue Task: Pupils are asked to consider the context of Dr. King's achievements on a world scale and could be asked to develop a set of criteria that separates out a national figure from a global figure.

Orange task: Pupils can be given roles before reading / listening to the extract. Roles for this might include white Americans living in the south, a foreign visitor, or a black civil rights activist.

Plenary
Ask pupils to think about other globally famous people. Using the criteria in the blue task how would they rank Dr. King's achievements and why?

Cross curricular links
Citizenship: The importance of civil rights.

ICT opportunities
Video and audio of Martin Luther King's speech can be accessed online. Go to www.heinemann.co.uk/hotlinks for links to the pages.

> 1 Ruling

1.8 How can you respond to terrorism?

1.8a Why is Tamerlan Satsayev afraid to go to school?

Learning objectives
- To learn about the effects of terrorism.
- To understand the causes and consequence of a historical incident.

Historical background
On 1 September 2004, a school in Besla, Chechnya, was attacked as children arrived for their first day of school. The events of the attack were initially confused, but the world soon came to hear about the conflict between Chechen rebels and the local Russian security forces, and questions were asked about how and why this could happen.

Teaching Activities and Learning Outcomes

Assessment opportunity

Establishing a sequence of key events and possible motivation leading to a historical incident.

Pupils will be able to

- describe the nature of an historical event using photographs and contemporary reports
- locate and sequence information from texts to produce an account of an event
- explain why people can hold differing points of view over a given event.

Starter

Ask pupils to make a list of things that they would want to take action in support of, or against. Introduce the idea of protest at different levels (local, national, international) and then what the nature of the protest might be. This can be used to place protest in a context. The final aspect to discuss is terrorism. Ask pupils where this sits in the scale of protest, if at all.

Development

Green task: Using **sources a** and **b** (page 60 of *History in Progress – Book 3*) pupils are encouraged to draw conclusions on the basis of limited media sources. Pupils could be asked to write down keywords as a way of accessing the pictures. The text in **source c** (page 60) gives more information, however pupils could be asked on a scale of one to ten whether they are sure of what happened in the school.

Blue task: Pupils sort through statements to develop a story, but at the same time need to be selective in order to produce a balanced account. To expand the exercise, ask pupils to use only certain sources in their writing; focus on the effect that limiting information has on the overall balance of the report.

Orange task: Pupils draw together differing accounts by focusing on an extreme view. There is scope here to use the sources and background to ask how such an opinion could be held, and to discuss things that people might ignore if the cause is strong enough.

Plenary

To gauge overall understanding ask the pupils a question to be answered by thumbs up / down or not sure e.g. 'If the cause is right ... there should be no limit to how you protest?'

Cross curricular links

Citizenship, Geography, Media

1 Ruling

1.8 How can you respond to terrorism?

1.8b Nelson Mandela: activist or terrorist?

Learning objectives
- To find out about the role of an individual in a struggle for justice.
- To decide on the status of an individual.

Historical background
The apartheid South African government, established after the Second World War, denied political freedoms on the basis of colour. After years of struggle, the African National Congress (ANC) and Nelson Mandela turned to sabotage as a means of protest for which Mandela was imprisoned for treason. While there the fight for his freedom focused attention on the injustice of the apartheid regime and led partly to its collapse.

Teaching Activities and Learning Outcomes

Assessment opportunity

Making judgements as to the significance of an individual to the achievement of a cause.

Pupils will be able to

- describe the nature of an individual's actions
- identify and explain how key moments contributed to the successful struggle against apartheid
- reach conclusions as to the status of an individual in a political struggle.

Starter

Explore as a class what pupils understand by the terms 'freedom fighter' and 'terrorist'. Ask students to give examples where possible. Alternatively provide students with a list of people throughout history that could be seen in this way (e.g. Guy Fawkes etc...).

Development

Green task: Pupils are asked to review information from **sources a–e** on pages 62–63 of *History in Progress – Book 3*. In order to ensure that pupils remain focused on the information, ask them to identify the most important source and to justify their answer. The second part of this task asks pupils to identify a turning point. To extend this exercise, ask pupils whether there were alternative points to 1961.

Blue task: Pupils use **sources a–l** on pages 62–63 to identify key moments of the apartheid struggle. A development of the exercise could be to give the pupils a figure for the number of key moments in order to either challenge, or help structure their answer.

Orange task: Pupils will need to revisit the definitions of 'terrorist' and 'freedom fighter' in order to make a judgement for this task. An extension that promotes classroom debate and discussion could be to ask the pupils to rank out of ten whether they believe the ANC was responsible for bringing an end to apartheid.

Plenary

Pupils focus on either the word 'freedom fighter' or 'terrorist' and place it in the middle of a spider diagram. They then choose words which relate to their chosen phrase and add them to the diagram.

Cross curricular links

Citizenship, Geography: Human rights and political systems in non-European countries.

> 1 Ruling

1.8 How can you respond to terrorism?

1.8c Why should we learn about terrorism?

Learning objectives
- To learn why people commit acts of terrorism.
- To be able to explain why acts of terrorism can be seen from different perspectives.

Historical background
The state of Israel gained its independence in 1948, when land that had previously been part of Palestine was given to the Jews to create their own land. The formation of the state was preceded by incidents of Jewish terrorism against British forces mandated to administer Palestine after the Second World War. In 1946 the King David Hotel in Jerusalem was blown up by a Jewish terrorist group and after years of conflict between the Palestinian Arabs and the Israelis, the Palestinians began to change the way they fought. In 2003 a popular restaurant was blown up in the Israeli coastal town of Haifa.

Teaching Activities and Learning Outcomes

Assessment opportunity

Developing an understanding that contemporary terrorism has complex causes.

Pupils will be able to

- describe, infer and propose questions as to the role of an individual in an historical context
- use source material to identify bias and reach conclusions as to the circumstances of an historical event
- assess critically the similarities and differences between two terrorist acts.

Starter

In order to provide a context, ask pupils to recall as many terrorist acts as they can. The attack on the Twin Towers is likely to feature highly in this discussion, so using pictures of incidents and asking students to place them in a date order can develop the exercise. Draw out why they can remember some incidents better than others, and what sort of experiences a person would need to have gone through if they remembered an incident from more than ten or twenty years ago.

Development

Green task: Pupils are asked to identify known facts before being encouraged to infer and then to raise questions about an individual simply on appearance. Care needs to be taken to challenge stereotypes during the exercise, which could be engaged with as an individual or whole class activity.

Blue task: Pupils study and interpret **sources a–d** (page 65, *History in Progress – Book 3*). Pupils need to consider the origin of the sources and whether this will have a bearing on how the incident is remembered / interpreted. This can be supported by asking pupils to look for key phrases or words that separate the two sources (and so changing the nature of the incident) and asking why these would have been included. An extension of the task could be to ask students to write a neutral version of the event.

Orange task: After identifying an interviewer, pupils can be asked to contribute questions in pairs or fours within the group, while the interviewees could be 'hot seated' to draw out facts and inferences before reaching a final conclusion.

Plenary

Ask pupils to work in pairs and write down two or three things that they feel they have learned which is new to them. The students choose one from each pair to feedback to the group.

Cross-curricular links

Citizenship, Media, Geography

1 Ruling

1.8 How can you respond to terrorism?

1.8d Ireland 1966 –1997: why did 'the Troubles' last so long?

Learning objectives
- To learn about terrorist activity in Ireland 1966–97
- To conclude the key factors in bringing to an end terrorist conflict

Historical background
In 1966, in the face of fierce opposition from the Protestant majority in Ulster, the Northern Irish government sought to introduce civil rights reforms for Catholics. Organised opposition groups soon clashed and a cycle of violence gripped the province that was to last for over 30 years, and was to leave nearly 4000 people dead.

Teaching Activities and Learning Outcomes

Assessment opportunity

Determining the cause and scope of a complex conflict.

Pupils will be able to

- explain why the nature of a conflict can determine how difficult the resolution is going to be.

Starter

Ask pupils to quickly make a list of all the reasons why people argue. This is likely to be focused on the individual level in the first instance, so pupils will need to be given a sense of context. Develop this by asking for reasons why groups of people argue, and then why countries might argue. From each of the three lists, ask pupils to identify one issue that is the most complex. A discussion can be developed about how these issues are resolved and what needs to be done to achieve that resolution.

Development

Green task: While pupils study **sources a** and **b** (page 66, *History in Progress – Book 3*), ask them to think where else such symbolic zoning of areas takes place (e.g. football stadiums), and what sort of feelings people have about belonging to one or the other area. Ask them to consider why murals are used rather than any other form of marker, and what might happen if the 'wrong' people crossed the line.

Blue task: The events of 'the Troubles' can be cut from **Worksheet 1.8d** in order to be grouped more easily. Pupils should be debriefed over what criteria they are using in order to create the groups or provided with categories to challenge their choices.

Orange task: Using the events of the conflict as cards, divide the group into two representing both sides of the conflict. Students should produce a rank order for both Catholics and Protestants to highlight the most significant moments for each of the communities of 'the Troubles'. Differences between the lists will highlight an increasing complexity as to what matters to each side, which can be the focus of a debate.

Plenary

Look back at the list of events in the Northern Ireland conflict. Ask pupils to select one event that would have made people think: 'No more'. Check the majority answer and explore reasons why, despite the tipping point, the conflict continued.

Cross-curricular links

Citizenship: Development of civil rights.

1 Ruling

1.8 How can you respond to terrorism?

Worksheet 1.8d Ireland 1966 – 1997: why did 'the Troubles' last so long?

4 Use the cards below to create categories around your central spider diagram.

6 As either a Catholic or a Protestant, use the cards to make a list in rank order of the most significant events of 'the Troubles' to your community ahead of possible peace negotiations.

Orange Marches
Parades by the Protestant Orange order through Catholic areas of Belfast resulted in heightened tension between the two communities.

Peace Movement 1976
This movement used mass demonstrations to show the desire of ordinary people on both sides of the divide for peace.

Bloody Sunday, 30 January 1972
During a civil rights march in Derry, 26 protesters were shot by the British army, 14 of whom died of their wounds.

The Peace Line
Wall-like barriers were built to separate Protestant and Catholic areas of the cities of Belfast and Londonderry

---

Brighton bombing, 12th October 1984
The IRA detonated a bomb at the Grand Hotel in Brighton where the Conservative government were at a conference. Although five people were killed, no government ministers died in the blast.

Internment 1971–1975
The policy of imprisonment without charge or trial of people accused of being members of illegal paramilitary (terrorist) groups. During the policy 1,874 Irish Nationalists were held, and 107 Ulster Unionists.

The Hunger Strikes, March 1981
Bobby Sansa led a protest with others in the Maze Prison, near Belfast, against being treated as 'ordinary prisoners' because he did not believe they were criminals. He said: 'We admit no crime unless, that is, the love of one's people and country is a crime.'

Birmingham pub bombings, 21 November 1974
Explosions in two pubs in Birmingham town centre killed 21 and injured 182. The IRA were blamed.

The RUC and B Specials 1970
The police and reserve police force were seen by the Catholic population as being pro-Protestant.

Civil Rights Demonstration 1968
A demonstration for Catholic civil rights in Londonderry was met with violence by the police.

1.8 How can you respond to terrorism?

1.8e Is there any solution to terrorism?

Learning objectives
- To consider the effectiveness of the methods of dealing with terrorism.
- To assess and reach conclusions as to possible solutions to terrorism.

Historical background
The attack on the World Trade Center in 2001 has become the stereotypical image associated with a terrorist attack, and yet terrorism comes in many forms and occurs for different reasons. How we respond to terrorism has become increasingly important, and the unit draws on different examples from the recent past to enable students to evaluate possible solutions.

Teaching Activities and Learning Outcomes

Assessment opportunity

Evaluating the impact of terrorism

Pupils will be able to

- describe the emotional impact of terrorism on the individual
- select from a range of options the most appropriate way to deal with terrorism
- reach conclusions as to the impact of terrorism on different people and institutions.

Starter

The twin towers example will be familiar to most pupils, so it might be useful to show them a lesser known terror example first to gauge uncluttered emotions to an event (in the form of a spider diagram) before using the twin towers. How are they similar / different, and what does this tell us about how people react to such incidents?

Development

Green task: Building on from the starter, pupils are asked to consider how attitudes change over time. Ask pupils to make a list of all the ways that people found out about the attack on the twin towers (from day one and then the following days). Would saturation media coverage change people's views? Identifying key words might be a useful way in to discussing the differing emotions.

Blue task: This task should be done as a snowball – individually at first before sharing with a pair then four etc. At each stage pupils should be given time to discuss their answer before increasing the size of the respondents. An extension of the task could bring in other acts of terrorism across time, e.g. the beginning of the First World War.

Orange task: For **task 5b**, you could break the class into three groups. Each group represents one of the three categories and has to make a case for terrorist acts affecting them more. For **task 7**, asking for an alternative solution to 'the full force of law' provides challenge.

Plenary

Give pupils two strips of paper on which they write down a question related to the work they have completed. Collect them in then select a few at random and pose them to the class. Ask the class to categorise the questions according to whether they feel there is a definite answer, a possible answer, or no answer. Homework might be set linked to the replies the students give.

Cross-curricular links

Citizenship, Geography, Media

Unit 1 Ruling

1.9 Making Connections: Who had the most effect?

Learning objectives
- To understand whom had the greater influence in bring about change – individuals or Governments?
- To understand the nature of change over a prolonged period.

Historical background

It would be difficult for someone plucked from 1900 to understand the world that existed in 2000, such was the nature of change throughout the twentieth century. Old certainties, built up over hundreds of years were swept away as advances in science and technology brought about new standards to the way that people lived and worked. But along with greater opportunities, the twentieth century also brought greater abilities to control people's lives. Where controlling ideas had once been the remit of leaders in a few countries, by the end of the century the ideas of the few could be seen to be having a worldwide effect, to which governments in their turn responded.

Teaching Activities and Learning Outcomes

Assessment opportunity

To reach conclusions on the basis of historical evidence

Pupils will be able to

- make decisions as to the importance of an event
- develop and express an opinion as to the significance of an event
- make links between events in order to reach a historically valid conclusion.

Starter

Diamond 9: Using the cards on **Worksheet 1.9 (1)** ask pupils to rank the events in terms of importance. There are more cards than needed, so the first task is to consider which of the events can be dismissed before building up the Diamond 9. Discussion can be developed around which cards were dismissed and why, before eventually debriefing the complete task.

Development

Green task: Model the placing of the first cross with the class before asking pupils to continue the task. Divide the x-axis into 1–5 and ask for a class decision about whether the 'success' of the suffragettes was more down to government or individuals. Debrief this carefully, challenging pupils' ideas and getting them to explain their answers in more than five words by using open questions e.g. 'So you mark it as... what was your thinking behind that?' [**Worksheet 1.9 (2)**].

Blue task: An alternative way of completing **task 4** would be to divide the class up into three groups and to use the available evidence to defend one position.

Orange task: The key to this task is to ask pupils to make links between the different events. Ask them to group the events 'into Individual influence' and 'government influence'. Check to see which events have been placed in each group before asking them to justify or make changes according to what they have heard in the discussion.

Plenary

Diamond 9 revisited: return to the cards that were used in the starter activity. In light of the discussion and main exercise ask the pupils to re-sort the cards. Debrief by asking whether they have used the same cards and whether any of the cards used have increased or declined in importance, and why?

Cross-curricular links

Citizenship, Geography

Unit 1 Ruling

Worksheet 1.9 (1) Who had the most effect?

In order to demonstrate that you have been able to reach a conclusion about the changes in the way that people were ruled during the twentieth century you will be asked to complete a 'Diamond 9.'

With a partner use the events cards below to reach a joint decision about which event during the century had the **most effect** on the way that people were ruled.

Before you start, you need to jointly make a decision about which events were important. To do this you will first need to get rid of some of the cards that you have. Be prepared to explain your choices.

- Place the event that you think was the most important at the top.
- Place the two events that are next in importance on the second line.
- Place the event that you have decided was the least important at the bottom, as this diagram shows.

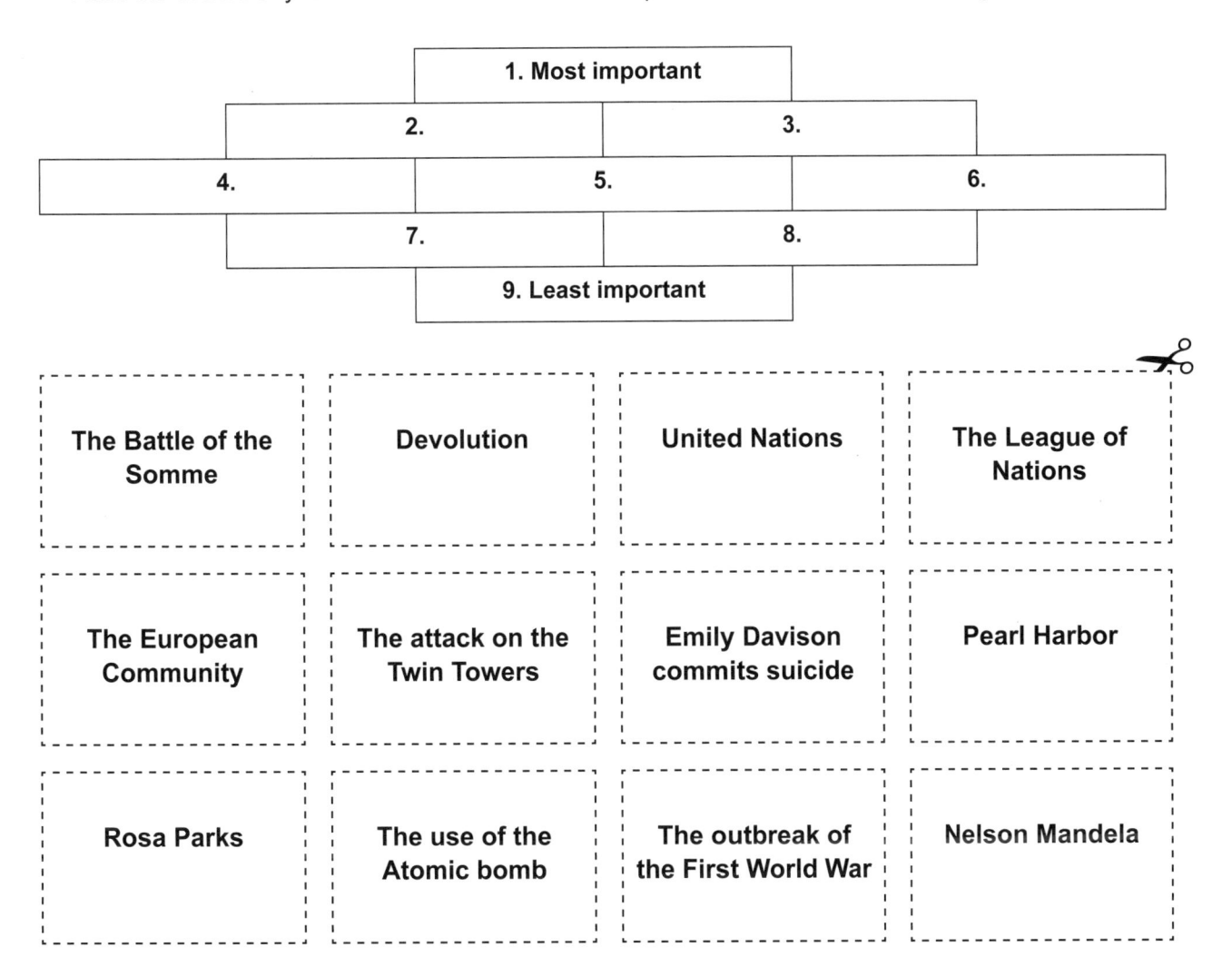

```
              1. Most important
         2.                    3.
    4.            5.                  6.
         7.                    8.
              9. Least important
```

The Battle of the Somme	Devolution	United Nations	The League of Nations
The European Community	The attack on the Twin Towers	Emily Davison commits suicide	Pearl Harbor
Rosa Parks	The use of the Atomic bomb	The outbreak of the First World War	Nelson Mandela

Compare your answers with those of another group

- Do they have the same cards as you? How did they choose their cards?
- In what ways have they ordered their cards and how are they similar or different to your order and why?
- What was your most important card? After listening to other members of your class would you change it and why?

1 Ruling

Unit 1 Ruling

Worksheet 1.9b (2) Making Connections: Who had the most effect?

Think back over the work you have completed in this unit. For each of the enquires you will need to think about whether it was the work of a single person, groups of people or governments that brought about change in the way people were ruled.

On the graph below make a judgement on how much of an effect took place in each enquiry by placing a cross on the graph to indicate your decision for each enquiry. When you have completed the graph compare your ideas with a partner. What does their graph look like and what reasons can you identify for the differences?

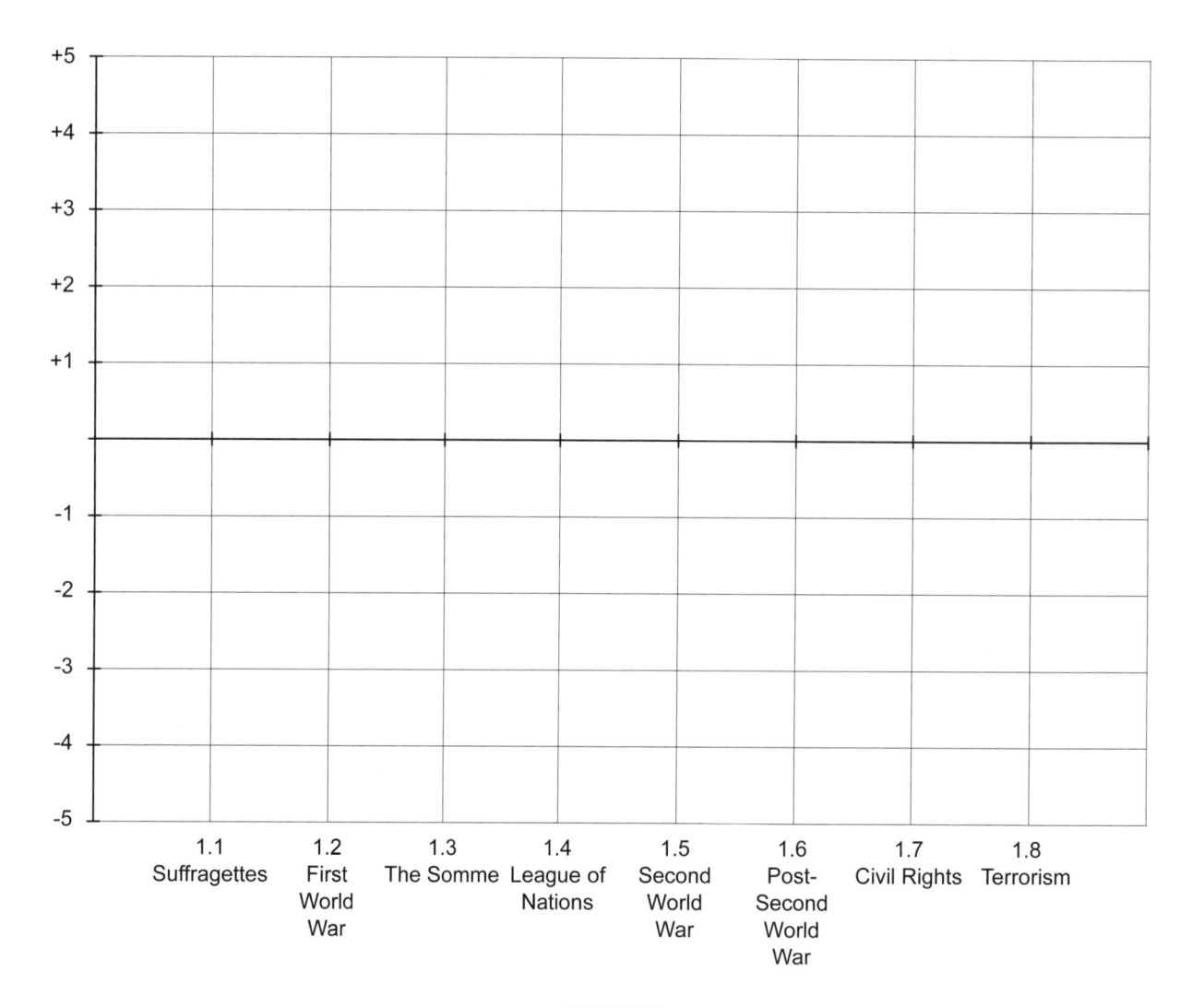

[Graph with y-axis from -5 to +5, and x-axis showing enquiries:
1.1 Suffragettes
1.2 First World War
1.3 The Somme
1.4 League of Nations
1.5 Second World War
1.6 Post-Second World War
1.7 Civil Rights
1.8 Terrorism

x-axis label: ENQUIRY]

Unit 1 Ruling

Assessment Unit 1

1.10 Assessment task 1: Why have there been different interpretations of Lenin?

Pupils will be able to

- explain why different interpretations exist
- evaluate which interpretations are more reliable or useful than others.

What the task is about

- The focus of this assessment task is interpretation.
- Ask pupils to read **sources a–d** on page 72 of *History in Progress – Book 3* before starting **tasks 1** and **2** (also on page 72). Guidance on how best to answer the questions is provided on page 73.
- The questions become more challenging. It is intended that pupils answer the questions on their own, using **Worksheet 1.10a (1–3)** as a guide if necessary. However, it is possible for the questions to be set as part of a group exercise with responses to **task 2d** to be fed back as part of a whole-class discussion.
- Pupils might wish to use the internet to research alternative interpretations of Lenin.
- Pupils move up the levels from Level 5 to 7 with successful completion of all questions. The assessment task is designed so that there is differentiation by task. A mark scheme is provided on **Worksheet 1.10 (4)**.
- This task can be undertaken either after completion of **Enquiry 1.4** or at the end of the unit.

1.11 Assessment task 2: Who had the most success in changing the way people were ruled in the twentieth century?

Pupils will be able to

- use examples of change and continuity to judge the significance of individuals in history
- make and test hypotheses as part of an investigation.

What the task is about

- The focus of this assessment task is comparing the significance of individuals who tried to change the way people were ruled in the twentieth century.
- The first step is for pupils to select the criteria against which they will judge the individuals. In addition to those listed in the textbook on page 74, other criteria might include 'did they achieve all of their goals?', 'did/do their contemporaries think of them as a success?', 'do their actions still affect the way people live today?'
- Following that, pupils explain which individual (or group in the case of the IRA) have had the most success when judged against the criteria they selected in **Step 1**. This could be done individually, in pairs or even snowballed into a whole class discussion.
- **Step 3** provides the opportunity to assess a piece of extended writing. It is intended that the pupils answer the question independently. Encourage pupils to plan their answer using the criteria and discussions from the first two steps.
- The pupils may use the internet to research further the overall success or impact of their chosen individual.
- Pupils move up the levels from Level 5 to 7 depending on the quality of their reasoning and explanation. The assessment task is designed so that there is differentiation by task. A mark scheme is provided on **Worksheet 1.11**.
- This exercise should be undertaken at the end of the unit.

1 Ruling

Unit 1 Assessment 1

Worksheet 1.10a (1) Why have there been different interpretations of Lenin?

1 Look at **sources a** and **b** below. Underline, or draw an arrow to different pieces of information given about Lenin. Compare the points you have picked out; use the points that agree in your answer.

a) Lenin was the creator of the tragedy of our era, the rise of dictatorships. He introduced to the twentieth century the practice of taking an ideology and forcing it on an entire society quickly and without mercy. He created a regime that erased historical memory and erased opposition. In his short career in power, from 1917 until his death in 1924, Lenin created a model for later dictators like Hitler and Chairman Mao.

b) Lenin justified dictatorship and terror. Lenin applauded strong leadership. Lenin convinced his party that his ideas were pure and always correct. He had a lasting impact upon communism in Russia and all over the world.

In what ways do **sources a** and **b** agree with each other?

_____
_____
_____

2 Look at **sources c** and **d** below. Underline, or draw an arrow to different pieces of information given about Lenin. Compare the points you have picked out; use the points that disagree in your answer.

c) Vladimir Lenin, a big, real man of this world, has passed away. His death is a painful blow to all who knew him, a very painful blow! But there is no force that could dim the torch he has raised for the people of the world. Never has there been a man who deserves more to be remembered forever by the whole world. His wisdom and his will are living. They are alive and working more successfully than anyone on Earth has ever worked before.

d) Lenin is a pathetic, bald little man, whose only use is to write endlessly. Lenin is also unpleasant. If he visited the countryside to investigate an outbreak of cholera, he would probably ban the disease and order the villagers who caught it to be punished! I hope that Lenin's power withers and fades away.

a) In what ways do **sources c** and **d** disagree about Lenin?

_____
_____
_____
_____

Unit 1 Assessment 1

Worksheet 1.10a (2) Why have there been different interpretations of Lenin?

2 continued

Now consider the provenance of the source in your answer; what is the nature, origin and purpose of the source? Again, use arrows to show where you can find the necessary information.

a) An American journalist's viewpoint

David Remnick is an American journalist; as Russian correspondent for the Washington Post, he lived in Moscow from 1988–92. **Source a** is his view of Lenin.

b) A modern British historian's viewpoint

Robert Service is Professor of Russian History at Oxford University. He has written many books about Lenin and about communism. **Source b** is his view of Lenin. He uses lots of new information that has been released by the Russian government.

b) Why do **sources a** and **b** differ in their interpretation of Lenin?

_____
_____
_____
_____

c) The viewpoint of one of Lenin's contemporaries

Maxim Gorky (1868–1936) was a Russian writer. He was a friend of Lenin's. He lived in Italy for many years, but, having been promised a mansion and the Order of Lenin medal by the Russian dictator Stalin, he returned to communist Russia. **Source c** gives his view of Lenin.

d) The view of another of Lenin's contemporaries

Before Lenin managed to enforce tight censorship in Russia, many people criticised his ideas and actions. **Source d** shows what Yevgeni Zamyatin, a member of the Socialist Revolutionary Party thought of him. He opposed Lenin's Bolshevik Party until he was banned in 1918.

c) Why do **sources c** and **d** differ in their interpretation of Lenin?

_____
_____
_____
_____

1 Ruling

Unit 1 Assessment 1

Worksheet 1.10a (3) Why have there been different interpretations of Lenin?

2 continued

d) Use the grid below before you answer this question. One point has been suggested for you.

Source	Tone of the content?	Points that show the author is reliable	Points that show the author is unreliable
a	Quite dramatic e.g. 'tragedy of our era'		
b			
c			
d			

Which interpretation of Lenin do you think is the most reliable?

_____
_____
_____
_____
_____
_____
_____
_____

1 Ruling

Unit 1 Assessment 1

Worksheet 1.10 (4) Why have there been different interpretations of Lenin?

How did you do?

Level 5: I was able to …

suggest reasons for different interpretations of Lenin	
evaluate sources to establish evidence	
select and use information including the correct historical words to support and structure my work.	

Level 6: I was able to …

begin to explain how and why different interpretations of Lenin have been made	
evaluate sources to establish evidence for my enquiry	
select, organise and use information, including the correct historical words, to produce structured work.	

Level 7: I was able to …

explain clearly how and why different interpretations of Lenin have been made	
begin to explain why views on the significance of Lenin have differed according to different viewpoints	
make judgements about the process of constructing history.	

Things I did well: _____

I need to learn more about: _____

One thing I could do to improve is: _____

I will do this by: _____

Pupil comment: _____

_____

_____

Teacher comment: _____

_____

1 Ruling

Unit 1 Assessment 2

Worksheet 1.11 Who had the most success in changing the way people were ruled in the twentieth century?

How did you do?

Level 5: I was able to ...

describe some of the changes people tried to make in the twentieth century	
suggest reasons for different interpretations of who was the most successful person	
select and use information including the correct historical words to support and structure my work.	

Level 6: I was able to ...

investigate historical problems and begin to ask my own questions as part of the enquiry	
evaluate sources to establish evidence for my enquiry	
produce well-organised work that used the correct historical words.	

Level 7: I was able to ...

explain how change and continuity differed over time in different places	
explain why different interpretations of the past have been made	
establish evidence for my enquiry by considering the provenance of sources	
produce well-organised work that uses carefully chosen information.	

Things I did well: _____

I need to learn more about: _____

One thing I could do to improve is: _____

I will do this by: _____

Pupil comment: _____

_____

_____

Teacher comment: _____

_____

2.1 Was there truly an Edwardian 'golden summer'?

2.1a What was life like in the pre-war years?

Learning objectives
- Find out what Britain was like in 1914.
- Use source material to explore the diversity of experience of living in Britain 1900-14 and to test the hypothesis that life in Britain was 'one long summer afternoon'.

Historical background
For many historians, the years before the Great War were halcyon days when the sun always shone and life resembled one long holiday. In many ways this was an understandable reaction to the carnage and brutality of the First World War, and historians, looking back over the horror, saw golden days before it. But it wasn't like that for everyone.

Teaching Activities and Learning Outcomes

Homework

Ask pupils to find a source that was created in Britain in the years between 1900 and 1914, and to write a few sentences explaining what it shows about life in Britain at that time. In this way, a class record of life in Britain 1900-14 can be made and could be entered in one big scrapbook.

Starter

A pupil (or the teacher) could take on the role of Agnes, and read out her memories that form **Source a**. She could then take questions from the class about her memories. Limit this to quick-fire questions and answers and then move on to the green task.

Development

Green task: The task could be taken as a whole class exercise and a composite picture of life in pre-1914 Britain built up. Alternatively, pupils could work as suggested in the green task and their findings taken as a plenary, with all their ideas being pulled together. Make it clear to them that they must limit themselves precisely to what they can see in the pictures: they are quarrying the images for information.

Blue task: This task builds upon the green task in a direct way. Here, pupils are working with the same three sources but in a different way. This time, they are using the images as a starting point of an investigation into life in Britain before 1914. The point of joining up with another pupil is not simply to sort out the 'best' questions but to focus on why they are 'best' – 'best' in that they will open up a line of investigation – and which questions won't lead anywhere. In this way pupil will be introduced to 'open' and 'closed' questions and should make use of this information in writing a note to their editor.

Orange task: This is a development of the blue task and requires pupils to consider in greater depth the questions they selected and to think about what they would like the outcomes to be. In this way, pupils will begin to understand how to structure an enquiry.

Plenary

Pulling it all together: quick-fire round on what it was really like to have lived in Britain before the First World War.

Cross-curricular links

Citizenship

> 2 Living and working

2.1 Was there truly an Edwardian 'golden summer'?

2.1b What were the threats to stability?

Learning objectives
- To find out about the issues that dominated the news in the summer of 1914.
- To investigate the significance of events in the summer of 1914.

Historical background
For many historians, the summer of 1914 was thought of as a 'golden' period. Images of hot summer days, peace and tranquillity dominate popular history and imagination. In one sense, the summer of 1914 was 'golden' in comparison to the carnage and brutality of the Great War which was to break out in August. But the image of a 'golden summer' is not perhaps as accurate a description. In the summer of 1914 Britain was bedevilled by a number of pressing political and social problems; industrial unrest was rife and the suffragettes were active. Ireland was on the verge of civil war as Ulster Unionists threatened to use force to resist Home Rule.

Teaching Activities and Learning Outcomes

Assessment opportunity

Investigating the significance of events.

Pupils will be able to

- sequence and summarise events
- discuss the seriousness of the events of the summer of 1914
- explain the significance of the summer of 1914.

Starter

Gimme five: ask the class for five words to describe the summer of 1914 as suggested by Lesson 2.1a. Look at **source a** (page 80, *History in Progress – Book 3*), does this source alter this impression?

Development

Green task: Pupils read the six reports on page 81 of *History in Progress – Book 3*. The first task asks them to put the reports in chronological order. They should then summarise each source. They can use the **Worksheet 2.1b (1)** to help complete this task.

Blue task: Pupils work in groups to discuss the issues and the extent to which they posed a threat to everyday life. **Task 2a–c** on can be used as starting points but groups can develop their discussion beyond these questions.

Orange task: Pupils complete a newspaper article which explains the significance of the events of 1914 emerging from the blue task discussions [**Worksheet 2.1b (2)**].

Plenary

Whole class discussion: How serious a threat to stability were the strikes, suffragettes and Irish question in the summer of 1914?

Cross-curricular links

Citizenship: Industrial unrest and direct action.

2.1 Was there truly an Edwardian 'golden summer'?

Worksheet 2.1b (1) What were the threats to stability?

1 Read each of the newspaper cuttings on page 81 of *History in Progress – Book 3*. Place the evidence in chronological order on the table below and then summarise each extract in twenty words or less.

Evidence	Summary

2 Living and working

2.1 Was there truly an Edwardian 'golden summer'?

Worksheet 2.1b (2) What were the threats to stability?

Use all of the information that you have to write an article about the truth of the summer of 1914. Your article will need a newspaper name, headline, picture and writing. You might want to illustrate it with adverts from the time.

The Post

2.2 How were the 'home fires' kept burning during the First World War?

2.2a How did the country keep going?

Learning objectives
- To find out how industry was kept going and how people were fed during the war.
- To use sources to show you understand why some people reacted as they did.

Historical background
The Defence of the Realm Act (DORA) meant that the government had powers to control the production and distribution of raw materials and manufactured goods. In reality, these were rarely used. The Ministry of Munitions was staffed at the top by businessmen loaned by their companies for the duration of the war. They were able to coordinate the needs of business with those of the state and reach a compromise on price and profit that was acceptable to both sides. For most of the war, people had enough to eat, but intensified submarine warfare brought problems and by April 1916, Britain had only four days' supply of sugar and nine weeks' supply of wheat left. Lord Devonport was replaced as food controller by Lord Rhondda in May 1917. Lord Rhondda set up an effective system of food rationing and distribution. George Prothero, President of the Board of Trade, established a system of local agricultural committees and by 1918, three million additional acres of land had been taken into cultivation.

Teaching Activities and Learning Outcomes

Homework

Ask pupils to find another First World War song or a First World War poem. What was its audience and what do they think its impact was?

Starter

Use a recording of the song in **source a** on page 82 of *History in Progress – Book 3*, and/or find the music and sing along. Ask how pupils felt as they were singing / listening. What might people at the time have felt? Move on to discussing the starter questions.

Development

Green task: Task 1 can be treated as a whole class exercise before moving on to a consideration of **sources c–e** (pages 82–83, *History in Progress – Book 3*). Encourage pupils to consider the origins as well as the content of the sources. The task could end with a whole class plenary, pulling all the ideas together.

Blue task: Begin with a plenary discussion as to what Milly's worries might be: a class list could be drawn up. There could then be discussion as to how much and how many of her concerns she should share with Fred, and whether she should focus on the positive and on keeping his spirits up. More able pupils might be encouraged to engage with who supported Milly.

Orange task: This is a development of the blue task and requires pupils to consider what is missing. They could start with their own letter and then swap with the letter of another pupil. Are the same issues missing from every letter? If not, why not?

Plenary

Ask two or three pupils that you know have different letters, to read them out loud to the class. Discuss what Fred's reaction to his letters might have been,

Cross-curricular links

PSHE, Economic awareness

2 Living and working

2.2 How were the 'home fires' kept burning during the First World War?

Worksheet 2.2a How did the country keep going?

Dear Fred

Para 1

Para 2

Para 3

Para 4

Your loving wife
Milly

74 © Pearson Education Ltd 2009: History in Progress – Planning and Resource Pack 3

2.2b How were the 'home fires' kept burning during the First World War?

2.2b What did people fear?

Learning objectives
- To find out how the Germans threatened mainland Britain.
- To explore the reactions of people and the government at home to the threats posed by the war.

Historical background

After May 1915, technological developments meant that naval bombardments of British east-coast towns were quickly superseded by aerial bombardments from zeppelins. Zeppelins required dark but fine nights for their raids. They hovered over their targets before dropping their bomb load. On 25 May 1917, the first raids using conventional aircraft occurred when Gotha GIV bombers based at Ghent launched a raid on Folkestone. Gothas could operate by day and night, even on moon-lit ones, and so were a more constant threat than Zeppelins. The British authorities had given little thought to co-ordinating air defence. A black-out for defended harbours was introduced in August 1914, and gradually extended; in July 1917, a basic air-raid warning system was introduced and public shelters were improvised.

Teaching Activities and Learning Outcomes

Assessment opportunity

Understanding the way in which the concept of total war was developed by the involvement of civilians; the innovative nature of aerial bombardment and the reaction of people and authority to it.

Starter

Quick fire round the class: What are you afraid of? Start the pupils off with some suggestions and don't linger to allow for teasing or scorn. Make it light-hearted.

Development

Green task: This task could be taken as a whole class activity, or take the first part as a plenary and then let the pupils work in pairs for the second part. Using **sources c** and **d** on page 84 of *History in Progress – Book 3*, pupils work in pairs to role play as Mrs Holcombe Ingleby and Sybil Morrison.

Blue task: This task involves a consideration of the nature of propaganda and what is, and is not, acceptable to use. Explain to pupils that during the Second World War, the government censored the use of a photograph of children killed in their school playground (see page 93 of *History in Progress – Book 3*). Why hasn't the image in **source e** been censored?

Orange task: Using the full version of the Proclamation (reproduced on **Worksheet 2.2b**), pupils consider the usefulness of such a proclamation, focusing on how sensible the instructions are. Pupils should also think about why the authorities wanted all copies returned.

Plenary

Extend the orange task by discussing with pupils whether they think the proclamation meant that the government was afraid, or simply being sensible. You could hold a class vote. Compare this proclamation to similar, more recent government information, such as the booklets that were sent to every UK household in 2004 regarding terrorist attacks.

Cross-curricular links

PSHE

2 Living and working

2.2 How were the 'home fires' kept burning during the First World War?

Worksheet 2.2b What did people fear?

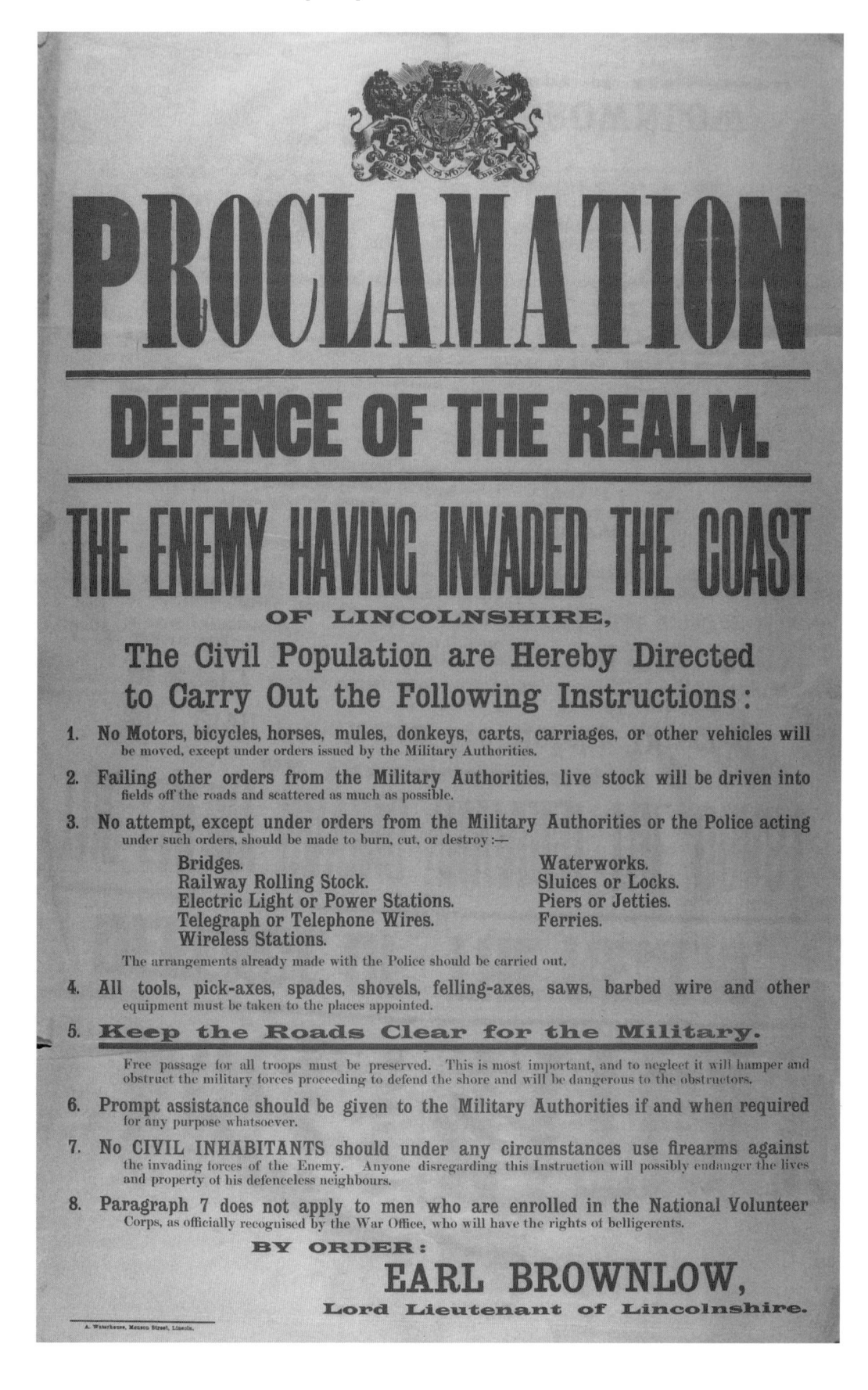

PROCLAMATION
DEFENCE OF THE REALM.

THE ENEMY HAVING INVADED THE COAST
OF LINCOLNSHIRE,

The Civil Population are Hereby Directed to Carry Out the Following Instructions:

1. No Motors, bicycles, horses, mules, donkeys, carts, carriages, or other vehicles will be moved, except under orders issued by the Military Authorities.
2. Failing other orders from the Military Authorities, live stock will be driven into fields off the roads and scattered as much as possible.
3. No attempt, except under orders from the Military Authorities or the Police acting under such orders, should be made to burn, cut, or destroy:—

   Bridges.
   Railway Rolling Stock.
   Electric Light or Power Stations.
   Telegraph or Telephone Wires.
   Wireless Stations.

   Waterworks.
   Sluices or Locks.
   Piers or Jetties.
   Ferries.

   The arrangements already made with the Police should be carried out.

4. All tools, pick-axes, spades, shovels, felling-axes, saws, barbed wire and other equipment must be taken to the places appointed.
5. **Keep the Roads Clear for the Military.**

   Free passage for all troops must be preserved. This is most important, and to neglect it will hamper and obstruct the military forces proceeding to defend the shore and will be dangerous to the obstructors.

6. Prompt assistance should be given to the Military Authorities if and when required for any purpose whatsoever.
7. No CIVIL INHABITANTS should under any circumstances use firearms against the invading forces of the Enemy. Anyone disregarding this Instruction will possibly endanger the lives and property of his defenceless neighbours.
8. Paragraph 7 does not apply to men who are enrolled in the National Volunteer Corps, as officially recognised by the War Office, who will have the rights of belligerents.

BY ORDER:
EARL BROWNLOW,
Lord Lieutenant of Lincolnshire.

2.2 How were the 'home fires' kept burning during the First World War?

2.2c Did everyone in Britain hate the Germans?

Learning objectives
- To find out how British people reacted to Germans living in Britain.
- To investigate whether everyone felt the same.

Historical Background
Roughly 35,000 Germans were living in Britain at the outbreak of the First World War, the third largest immigrant group after the Irish and Jews. Spy-stories abounded and soon the Germans became the object of suspicion and attack. In reality, the authorities were monitoring some twenty-two known German spies. One escaped back to Germany, fourteen were imprisoned of which eleven were subsequently executed. The public demand for the internment of Germans grew, and about 30,000 were interned, mostly on the Isle of Man. All immigrants were compelled to register under the Aliens Registration Act, August 1914.

Teaching Activities and Learning Outcomes

Homework

Find out who Edith Cavell was, and what she did. Were the authorities right to execute her?

Starter

Ask pupils to look at the list of name changes and pick out which they think are the silliest and the most serious. Go around the class asking for their choices and compare them. Ask pupils to explain their choices and then consider why the changes were made when everyone knew the original name.

Development

Green task: Pupils are asked to compare a photograph and a written source (**sources a** and **b** on page 86 of *History in Progress – Book 3*). Encourage them to go behind the surface features and consider such things as attitudes. **Worksheet 2.2c** may help pupils clarify their thoughts.

Blue task: Pupils are asked to consider and compare motives by studying a photographic and a written source (**sources c** and **d** on page 87 of *History in Progress – Book 3*). They then need to consider an alternative point of view. The first part of the task could be undertaken in pairs or small groups; the final part should be an individual exercise.

Orange task: Using **sources a–d** on pages 86 and 87 of *History in Progress – Book 3*, pupils consider the origin of sources and their reliability. Who was the intended audience? Was the photograph posed? Why? You might like to refer to the skills analysis in the Skillsbank (pages 186–189 of *History in Progress – Book3*).

Plenary

Back to the start: Have a class plenary to review and evaluate work done over the enquiry. **Worksheet 2.2c** may help with this.

Cross-curricular links

Citizenship, PSHE, Geography

2 Living and working

2.2 How were the 'home fires' kept burning during the First World War?

Worksheet 2.2c Did everyone in Britain hate the Germans?

1 Use the table below to sort the similarities and differences between **source a** and **source b** on page 86 of *History in Progress – Book 3*.

How source a differs from source b	Similarities between sources	How source b differs from source a

Back to the Start

Choose key events that you have studied through the course of this enquiry and list them in the table below. Then rate how successfully you think the British people coped on the home front with regards to these events.

Event	Rating

2.3 How did people in Britain survive the Second World War?

2.3a What did people fear this time?

Learning objectives
- To find out how people at home tried to keep themselves safe.
- To explore the differences in people's reactions to the threats posed by the war.

Historical background
Anderson and Morrison shelters were available for people to try to keep themselves safe in their own homes. People living in houses with cellars used those, otherwise they sheltered under the stairs and hoped for the best. Public shelters were built on street corners, bus stations, market places etc., to provide shelter for people away from home. After initial opposition, people in London were allowed to use the tube as deep shelters and eventually they were equipped with bunk beds and chemical toilets. In May 1940, the Local Defence Volunteers (LDV) were formed. Thousands of men not eligible for military service joined up. Despite some initial problems with the 'Home Guard' (such as equipping them and outlining their role in the event of an invasion), the LDV did fulfil a useful function in learning how to defend Britain against potential invasion and also in making people feel safer.

Teaching Activities and Learning Outcomes

Homework

Talk to someone who was alive during the Second World War (start with grandparents or older neighbours). Ask what they can remember about air-raid shelters and/or the Home Guard. Share these memories with the rest of the class and make a Second World War memory scrapbook.

Starter

Hold a quick-fire recap on what people were afraid of during the First World War (answers could include: death at the Front, shortages, zeppelins, Gotha bombing raids etc.). Make the transition from the air-raids of the First World War to those of the Second World War and then ask pupils to study the photograph in **source a** (page 88 of *History in Progress – Book 3*) and work on the starter questions

Development

Green task: The first part of the task could be taken as a whole class exercise to get ideas flowing as to what the two children could be thinking. Then move to writing individual diary entries. Pupils may find **Worksheet 2.3a** helpful.

Blue task: Ask some of the pupils to read out their diary entries (aim to get a range of different views) before moving on to read the sources. Discuss with the class the comparisons between their imagined opinions and those of the authors who lived through it. The whole task could be conducted orally and pupils could then move to writing.

Orange task: Churchill's speech (**source g** on page 91 of *History in Progress – Book 3*) could be read out and the first task could be taken as a plenary. Pupils are then asked to read **sources h** and **i** (also page 91) and complete the **tasks 4** and **5** individually.

Plenary

Pupils who have completed the third orange task could be asked to read out their responses (no more than three) and these could be used as the basis of a whole class discussion.

ICT opportunities

Pupils could write their diary entries up on computer, or even as an online diary (blog).

2 Living and working

2.3a How did people in Britain survive the Second World War?

Worksheet 2.3a What did people fear this time?

MY DIARY

My name is

My age is

I am keeping this diary hidden in my bunk in our family's Anderson shelter. I am writing down my private thoughts as the raids go on outside.

Thursday

Saturday

Tuesday

Wednesday

2.3 How did people in Britain survive the Second World War?

2.3b How were children kept safe?

Learning objectives
- To discover how the government hoped to keep the children safe during the Second World War.
- To use sources to explore the reactions of some children and the families with whom they stayed.

Historical background

Between 1939 and 1944, there were four major evacuations of people from the cities to the countryside to keep them safe from Luftwaffe bombing raids. The first evacuation took place on 1 September 1939, two days before the declaration of war. 60% of evacuated children returned home by January 1940, because there were no bombings. The second evacuation was in June 1940, after the fall of France. In the same year, 100,000 children were evacuated on 7 September. Then in June 1944, in response to V1 and V2 rocket attacks, 1 million women, children, elderly, and disabled people were sent into the countryside. Billeting officers found host families for the evacuees but not all took care to match families with evacuees, and most host families were unprepared for the inner city children (and their mothers) who arrived. By the end of the war, around 3.5 million people had experienced evacuation. Additionally, some children were sent to families in Canada, the USA, South Africa, Australia and the Caribbean.

Teaching Activities and Learning Outcomes

Assessment opportunity

Understanding of the motives of central government, the way in which this was put into action with regard to evacuation and the impact this had on the children involved.

Starter

Ask the class if anyone has been to a sleep-over. Ask those who have who they stayed with, how long they stayed, why they went. Aim for a majority of responses that agree that staying away, with friends or family, was usually for fun. Now ask them to imagine that they are being sent away, that the government has persuaded their parents that they should live with complete strangers. Now ask them to study the photograph in **source a** on page 92 of *History in Progress – Book 3* and work on the questions with it.

Development

Green task: The first part of this task could be taken as a whole class activity, with pupils then working in pairs to devise a better system of evacuation. Remind them that this is wartime and speed is of the essence.

Blue task: Working in pairs, or individually, pupils identify and list the range of problems experienced by evacuees and their host families. **Worksheet 2.3b** may help them with this. The second part of the task could be written up as a mini-essay, or it could form the basis of a class debate.

Orange task: Pupils work individually on **task 4**, producing a paragraph at most. For **task 5**, pupils work in pairs with one making out a case for publication and the other for censorship.

Plenary

Class discussion on what thoughts and arguments pupils have come up with in their pairs.

Cross-curricular links

English, PSHE

2.3 How did people in Britain survive the Second World War?

Worksheet 2.3b How were children kept safe?

Use this table to help order and sort the problems you believe evacuees and their host families encountered. Use **sources c–f** (page 93 of *History in Progress – Book 3*) to gather information.

	Evacuees	Host families
Problem 1		
Problem 2		
Problem 3		
Problem 4		
Problem 5		
Problem 6		
Problem 7		
Problem 8		
Problem 9		
Problem 10		

2 Living and working

2.3 How did people in Britain survive the Second World War?

2.3c How were people fed?

Learning objectives
- To find out how food and clothing were rationed during the Second World War.
- To understand how the government tried to help all the people to be fed and clothed.

Historical background

Diverting manpower and production into the war effort meant that consumer goods of all kinds became scarce. Food production was particularly difficult because the UK was dependent on supplies from overseas. Rationing was therefore imposed through a 'points' system and prices were controlled. Ration books and clothing coupons were issued to all, with some adjustments to meet special requirements. By and large the public accepted rationing and, although a black market flourished, it never seriously undermined the system. Many people ate in work canteens at lunchtime and the government set up a chain of 'British restaurants' where wholesome meals could be obtained cheaply. Generally, the imposition of a balanced diet kept the nation healthy and the main complaint was monotony and boredom with the menus that were possible. Shortages varied throughout the war and entitlement did not mean that a particular foodstuff was available. Bread, potatoes, coffee, vegetables, fruit and fish were never rationed though the availability of the last three varied. Allotments flourished and parks and gardens were given over to food production

Teaching Activities and Learning Outcomes

Homework

Ask your family, friends and neighbours if they grow their own fruit and vegetables. Find out where these are grown (gardens, balconies, allotments?) What is being grown? Why?

Starter

Pick up from, or introduce, the homework task by asking whether it is better to grow your own fruit and vegetables or to buy from the supermarket. What are the problems involved? Ask pupils to look at the 'Dig for Victory' poster in **source a** on page 95 of *History in Progress – Book 3* and discuss the questions.

Development

Green task: This could easily be merged with the starter and could be a whole class oral exercise.

Blue task: The first part of the task (**task 2a–c**) could be done orally with the whole group, or pupils could work in pairs, sharing ideas with the class after a short period of time. Hand out **Worksheet 2.3c (1)** which has a full reproduction of the menu in **source d** on *History in Progress – Book 3*. The second task should be undertaken individually, **Worksheet 2.3c (2)** may aid them in this.

Orange task: Pupils use **sources a–e** (pages 94–95 of *History in Progress – Book 3*) as well as their own thoughts and notes throughout the lesson to prepare a presentation promoting rationing. This could be individual or group work.

Plenary

Back to the start: Hold a class plenary on this task to kick start inspiration for the letter or conversation.

Cross-curricular links

Food technology / cookery, Economic awareness, PSHE, English

2.3 How did people in Britain survive the Second World War?

Worksheet 2.3c (1) How were people fed?

MONDAY

Breakfast (each day): Porridge or breakfast cereal. Fruit. Toast. Marmalade. Eggs occasionally. Milk or milky tea.

Dinner: Vegetable soup or Jacket sausages. Raisin dumplings with golden syrup.

Tea-Supper: Blackberry bake. Wholemeal bread and butter. Cocoa.

TUESDAY

Dinner: Mutton pie. Jacket potatoes. Baked apple.

Tea-Supper: Macaroni cheese. Bread and butter. Fruit. Milk or tea.

WEDNESDAY

Dinner: Braised beef. Vegetables. Chocolate blancmange.

Tea-Supper: Scrambled eggs on toast. Stewed dried apricots. Milk drink.

THURSDAY

Dinner: Baked marrow. College pudding.

Tea-Supper: Vegetable casserole. Bread and jam. Tea or fruit-juice drink.

FRIDAY

Dinner: Bombay rice. Cabbage. Golden apples.

Tea-Supper: Vegetable salad on lettuce. Wholemeal bread and butter. Rice pudding.

SATURDAY

Dinner: Liver casserole. Mashed potatoes. Greens. Milk jelly.

Tea-Supper: Bread and butter pudding. Fruit.

SUNDAY

Dinner: Beef, carrots and dumplings. Greens. Sponge pudding.

Tea-Supper: Cheese and tomato sandwiches. Cake. Milk drink.

2.3 How did people in Britain survive the Second World War?

Worksheet 2.3c (2) How were people fed?

3 Use the table below to compare your diet now with diets of 1942.

	Now	1942
Breakfast		
Lunch / dinner		
Tea / supper		
Snacks		

Which is more balanced?

Reasons?

Which is healthier?

Reasons?

Which do you prefer?

Reasons?

2 Living and working

2.3 How did people in Britain survive the Second World War?

2.3d Taking it further! The end of the war in Europe

Learning objectives
- To use given sources as evidence for reactions to the ending of the war in Europe.

Historical background
From the beginning of 1945, it became clear that the end of the war was in sight. In June 1944, allied troops had invaded Europe (known as D-Day) and there had been steady advances since that date. On 2 May 1945, the German forces in Italy surrendered. A day later German forces in Northern Germany, Denmark and the Netherlands surrendered to Field Marshal Montgomery, and the final document of unconditional surrender was signed at general Dwight Eisenhower's headquarters in Reims on 7 May. This was the end of the war in Europe.

Teaching Activities and Learning Outcomes

Assessment Opportunity

Pupils will be working with source material, making inferences and backing their views with evidence and so this is an ideal opportunity for the assessment of pupils' ability at source evaluation.

Starter

Ask pupils to look at the photograph of Gunner Hector Murdoch returning home (**source a** on page 96 of *History in Progress – Book 3*). Quick-fire round the class: one word to describe the photograph.

Development

Task 1: Ask pupils to study **sources a–c** on page 96 of *History in Progress – Book3*, and to make some notes about each one to help with the next task.

Task 2: In order to answer this task effectively, pupils will need to consider everything they have learnt throughout the enquiry regarding sources and how to evaluate them. You could refer them to the Skillsbank on pages 186–189 of *History in Progress – Book 3*. It is important for pupils to support their views with evidence and clear explanations.

Task 3a and b: Pupils will now be evaluating a different kind of source than previously, and they should bear this in mind when dealing with it. As with the previous task, the quality of support they give for their answers is what is important.

Plenary

Use **task 3** as a plenary and ask the pupils to consider both the message and the date of publication. How powerful is the image and message?

2 Living and working

2.4 Why do genocides happen?

2.4a How did the Nazis try to kill all European Jews?

Learning objectives
- To explore what happened to Jews under Nazi control.
- To use pictorial information to investigate a problem.

Historical background

On 30 January 1933, Adolf Hitler was appointed Chancellor of democratic Germany. Through a combination of violence, propaganda, and legal loopholes he effectively became dictator of Germany by the end of March 1933. He was a racist and an anti-Semite, but only approved anti-Semitic measures that would not damage the economy, or upset the elites he needed to please. By 1938, his regime was secure and anti-Semitic measures became more radical. Kristallnacht (Night of Broken Glass) on 9 and 10 November is often considered a watershed. Historians view the Nazi regime as a powerful police state; while fear was certainly a powerful motive for conformity, it has become increasingly clear that the size of the terror network was not as extensive as once thought. The Gestapo (secret police) often relied on denunciations for 'race crimes' (infringements of the 1935 Nuremburg Laws). Propaganda and 'co-ordination' (Nazification) of peoples' work, social and private lives must have encouraged anti-Semitism.

Teaching Activities and Learning Outcomes

Assessment opportunity

Analysing and explaining the reasons for, and results of, historical events, situations and changes; evaluating sources used as part of a historical enquiry.

Pupils will be able to

- extract relevant information from a range of pictorial sources
- evaluate which sources offer the best evidence for finding out about Nazi anti-Semitic actions.

Starter

In pairs, pupils look at **source a** (page 98, *History in Progress – Book 3*). Ask them to feedback their theories to the class. If the suggestion of 'being ordered' arises, ask pupils to consider why someone might be ordered to shoot a defenceless woman and child. Is it a one-off incident or part of a wider campaign? Is this sort of thing inevitable in all wars?

Development

Green task: Pupils could complete this task individually or in pairs. **Worksheet 2.4a** will help structure their answers to **tasks 1a** and **1b**.

Blue task: Pupils could discuss this in pairs before completing the task individually. Give the class some criteria with which to make their decisions: how reliable is the source as evidence of what the Nazis were doing? How typical or representative is this source? How informative is the source content? **Worksheet 2.4a** could be used to structure these answers.

Orange task: Encourage pupils to use the categories from **task 1** to organise their paragraphs. Their answers to **task 2** will help explain the various pressures which most encouraged anti-Semitism.

Plenary

Many Germans have claimed that they were 'brainwashed' by the propaganda of the Nazi government to be anti-Semitic. Have a class debate on how convincing pupils find this argument. Ask pupils to consider the power of advertising and the media in their lives today.

Cross-curricular links

Citizenship: The nature of the relationship between the state, the media, the law and the individual.

2 Living and working

2.4 Why do genocides happen?

Worksheet 2.4a How did the Nazis try to kill all European Jews?

1 Look at **sources b–e** (page 99, *History in Progress – Book 3*). Use details from each source to explain which of the following methods for encouraging anti-Semitism the source best shows:

- propaganda
- use of the law to exclude Jews from public life
- fear of arrest for those who disagree with Nazi views
- removal of Jews from Germany.

Source	Method	Evidence for this from the source
b		
c		
d		
e		

2 Look again at **sources b–e**. This time, use the content of the source and the provenance of the source (its nature, origin and purpose) to decide which two sources give the best evidence that the Nazis were trying to make ordinary Germans hate Jews.

Best sources are:	What we can learn from the content	Things about the provenance of the source that make it useful

2 Living and working

2.4 Why do genocides happen?

2.4b Who was to blame for the 'Final Solution'?

Learning objectives
- To investigate who was responsible for the 'Final Solution'.
- To use written sources to support an argument.

Historical background

Historians are divided into those who see the 'Final Solution' (the industrial murder of Jews, gypsies and homosexuals in gas chambers) as always planned by Hitler, and those who see it as the result of a range of pressures and concerns. Hitler spoke of putting '10,000 Jewish defilers under poison gas' in his 1924 political testament *Mein Kampf*, and the 'destruction of European Jewry' at his 1939 speech at the Berlin Sportpalast. Most historians now accept that Hitler was dealing with grand visions rather than detailed plans. Hitler certainly intended to clear Europe of Jews, but their murder in gas chambers seems to have resulted from pressure to clear the overcrowded ghettos of Nazi-occupied Poland, concerns over the demoralising impact on German soldiers of shooting women and children, and the expertise of gassing developed from 1938, as part of the euthanasia programme. The decision to gas as many Jews as possible was probably made in the late summer of 1941. The Wannsee Conference of 20 January 1942, merely confirmed the details of the plan to the various branches of the Nazi administration.

Teaching Activities and Learning Outcomes

Assessment opportunity

Analysing and explaining the reasons for, and results of, historical events, situations and changes; understanding how historians and others use sources to form interpretations of historical events.

Pupils will be able to

- extract relevant information from a range of written sources
- use evaluated evidence to support or criticise an interpretation of an historical problem.

Starter

As a class, read through the first paragraph on page 100 of *History in Progress – Book 3* and discuss the starter question. The most logical answer is 'to kill the Jews', but ask pupils to recall aspects of anti-Semitism from the previous enquiry that underpinned this goal. Many leading Nazis opposed sending the Jews to Siberia: they feared that a new race of 'super-Jews' would evolve and return to exact revenge.

Development

Green task: Pupils complete **task 1a** by themselves before discussing the letter as a class. Explain to the pupils that the content of the letter is shocking, but it is part of an original letter found by the Red Army at Auschwitz (the whole letter is far too graphic to include in its entirety in the textbook). There is a copy of the letter on **Worksheet 2.4b (1)**. **Task 1b** can be done individually or in pairs. **Worksheet 2.4b (2)** will help structure their research.

Blue task: Working individually or in pairs, pupils pick out key information from the sources. **Worksheet 2.4b (2)** will help structure their research.

Orange task: Encourage pupils to look back over their work for the previous tasks, and the last enquiry, in order to decide which statement they agree with more. Emphasise that pupils need to use strong evidence gathered from the sources to support their interpretation and to attack the other interpretation. You could have a class debate after an initial period of brainstorming in order to model some possible ways of answering the question. The final written response could be set as a piece of homework.

Plenary

Class debate: Was Goldhagen right to blame extreme German anti-Semitism for the Holocaust?

2 Living and working

2.4 Why do genocides happen?

Worksheet 2.4b (1) Who was to blame for the 'Final Solution'?

1 Read though Zalmen Gradowski's letter. As you read, underline or draw arrows to show where
- he has used powerful words or images
- he explains his motives for writing such a letter.

> Dear reader,
>
> I am writing these words in the hour of my greatest despair. I hope that you will take revenge on the murderers! You must give my life some meaning! In the large room, deep underground, a sign tells the victims to undress because they are now in the 'showers'. They look terrified; they know, they understand: they will be wiped out. It will be as if they were never born. These are not real showers: not water but gas comes out of them. After the gassing, the dead bodies are dragged from the tangle to the crematoria. Children are piled up like logs at the side then added afterwards, thrown on top of each pair of adults on an iron stretcher. The furnace is opened and the stretcher pushed in. The hair catches light first. The skin swells and blisters, bursting open after a few seconds. Arms and legs twist, veins and nerves seize up and cause the limbs to jerk. By now the whole body is on fire, the skin splits open, fat spills out and you hear the fire sizzle. The stomach bursts. The intestines pour out and within a few minutes no trace remains. The whole process takes 20 minutes, a body, a world, is reduced to dust...

2.4 Why do genocides happen?

Worksheet 2.4b (2) Who was to blame for the 'Final Solution'?

2 Look at **sources b–h** (pages 102–103, *History in Progress – Book 3*).

- Use information in the sources to make a list of people who helped to carry out the 'Final Solution'.
- Complete the table by suggesting whether the source better supports the conclusion that Nazi leaders or ordinary Germans were largely to blame.

Source	People who helped carry out the 'Final Solution'	Who was to blame: Nazi leaders or ordinary Germans?
b		
c		
d		
e		
f		
g		
h		

3 Look again at **sources b-h** on pages 102–103. This time explain why the content and the provenance (its nature, origin and purpose) of the source might lead historians to reach different conclusions about who was to blame.

Source	Confusing content?	Problems with the provenance?
b		
c		
d		
e		
f		
g		
h		

> 2 Living and working

2.4 Why do genocides happen?

2.4c Why did the Hutus try to kill all the Tutsis?

Learning objectives
- To investigate reasons why the 1994 genocide happened in Rwanda.
- To weigh up the importance of different causes of the genocide.

Historical background
There is still debate over the origins of the Hutus and Tutsis. Many scholars support the idea that the Tutsis originated near modern Ethiopia and migrated to Rwanda later than the Hutus. Others argue that differences in height can be explained by the different diets and lifestyles of the cattle-herding Tutsis and subsistence-farming Hutus. Wherever their origins, there has been so much intermarriage over the years that it is generally difficult to tell Hutu from Tutsi. Both groups now refer to themselves as 'Rwandans'.

Teaching Activities and Learning Outcomes

Assessment opportunity

Analysing and explaining the reasons for, and results of, historical events, situations and changes; making and testing hypotheses about the past in pairs and as part of a larger team.

Pupils will be able to

- prioritise a range of causes that explain the 1994 genocide in Rwanda
- create and defend an argument about the most important factors that caused the 1994 genocide in Rwanda.

Starter

Hold a class discussion on the starter question. Make a note of some of the groups mentioned and the ways in which they define themselves. Ideas about dress, physical appearance, activities, language, and attitudes should emerge. Keep these ideas on the board to help pupils with **task 1**.

Development

Green task: Pupils work individually or in pairs. The statement is reproduced on **Worksheet 2.4c (1)**.

Blue task: As a class, read through all the cards to ensure that pupils understand the content. Discuss criteria for deciding which cards are the most important in explaining why the genocide happened. You could suggest that perhaps some cards are of equal importance (using the idea of necessary but not sufficient). Pupils could either physically manipulate copies of the cards from **Worksheet 2.4c (2)**, or they could use the table on **Worksheet 2.4c(1)** to keep a track of how their hypothesis develops, and how far they were able to defend their initial hypothesis.

Orange task: Pupils complete these tasks individually. Encourage pupils to make use of the discussions they had while carrying out the previous task. Both questions could be answered with a single, detailed paragraph; alternatively, **task 3a** could be used as a plenary with **task 3b** set as a homework essay. Pupils should be encouraged to dedicate a paragraph to each card, building from the least important to the most important if this is used for homework.

Plenary

Give pupils time to look back over their work in the previous two enquiries, and then ask them to vote on whether they think there are more similarities or differences. Ask pupils to justify their decisions before voting again in the light of these justifications.

Cross-curricular links

PSHE: Relationships between different groups within a community and the negative consequences of tension and hatred.

2.4 Why do genocides happen?

Worksheet 2.4c (1) Why did the Hutus try to kill all the Tutsis?

1 Look at Janet Uylsabye's statement below. Pick out the reasons why she thought the Hutus wanted to murder her. You could underline or draw arrows to highlight the reasons.

> Hutus think Tutsis are too tall and delicate; that they keep all the cattle and money for themselves rather than work hard on the farms like the Hutus. Hutus feared that the Tutsis would rise up and kill them. When the Hutus came to the school, grandmother told us to be quiet and to lie down. I lay down between a lot of grown ups. I saw them kill my sister and grandmother with machetes. I crawled under my grandmother's dead body to hide. All the screaming stopped and the only voices I could hear were those of the killers. One killer said, 'I think that little thing is still alive'. Another said, 'I will cut her and if she does not move she is dead'. That was when I felt a heavy blow on the back of my neck.

2 Use the table below to record the order of importance for the cards that help to explain why the 1994 genocide in Rwanda happened (pages 104–105, *History in Progress – Book 3*).

Card	Order of importance (pairs)	Order of importance (fours)	Order of importance (eights)	Order of importance (class)
1: The Belgians				
2: President Habyarimana (Hutu)				
3: The RPF (Tutsi)				
4: The akazu (Hutu)				
5: The United Nations (UN)				

2 Living and working

2.4 Why do genocides happen?

Worksheet 2.4c (2) Why did the Hutus try to kill all the Tutsis?

Card 1:

The Belgians

Rwanda was a Belgian colony from 1919 until 1962. The Belgians believed that the Tutsis were racially superior. In 1931, they introduced identification cards that said whether a Rwandan was Hutu or Tutsi. Only the Tutsis could work for the Belgians and the Hutus became jealous. When the Belgians left, the Hutus rose up and took power for themselves.

Card 2:

President Habyarimana (Hutu)

President Habyarimana had ruled Rwanda since 1973. He did not let the Tutsis in neighbouring countries return home. He gave all the best jobs to Hutus. In 1993, he signed the Arusha Accords, an agreement to share power with the Tutsis, and to merge the Rwandan Patriotic Front (RPF) and the Rwandan Army. He was killed on 6 April 1994 when his plane was shot down. The genocide started the next day.

Card 3:

The RPF (Tutsi)

In 1962, many Tutsis fled to neighbouring countries where they were forced to live in refugee camps. In 1988, when it became clear that they would not be allowed home, the Tutsis formed their own army, the Rwandan Patriotic Front (RPF) to fight their way back home. In October 1990, the RPF started the attacks on Rwanda that eventually forced Habyarimana to sign the Arusha Accords. Many Hutus began to fear the return of Tutsi power.

Card 4:

The akazu (Hutu)

Akazu means 'little hut'. It was the name given to the small group of President Habyarimana's friends and relatives who controlled all the powerful jobs in Rwanda. In 1990 they started to organise the interahamwe. Between 1992 and 1994, the interahamwe leaders imported a huge number of machetes. They were handed out by local mayors in the villages. The mayors also drew up lists of local Tutsis. In 1993, the akazu set up the RTLM radio station. On 7 April 1994, the DJ said, 'The cockroaches (Tutsis) have killed the President. You must take your spears, clubs, guns, swords, stones, everything - hack them, those cockroaches!'

Card 5:

The United Nations (UN)

Romeo Dallaire, the UN General in Rwanda, reported that the interahamwe were making lists of Tutsis to murder. He asked for permission to seize their guns. Kofi Annan, his boss at the UN headquarters told him to do nothing, but keep watching. On April 21, the UN evacuated all white people, and reduced their number of troops in Rwanda from 2,568 to 270.

2.4 Why do genocides happen?

2.4d Taking it further!: Are genocides unique?

Learning objectives
- To use hypotheses derived from previous enquiries in framing an investigation into a different problem of historical causation.

Historical background

Far from the Holocaust being the 'genocide to end all genocides', there have been many genocides throughout the twentieth century. The key question here is why genocides, despite international agreement since 1948 on what they are, and the need for action to prevent them from happening, have occurred with depressing frequency. There is an ongoing argument among History teachers about how the Holocaust should be taught. Disagreements centre on whether or not it should be thought of as a unique event in human history.

Teaching Activities and Learning Outcomes

Assessment opportunity
Analysing and explaining the reasons for different genocides; identifying, selecting and using a range of historical sources to make and test hypotheses about the past.

Pupils will be able to
- devise areas of comparison between different genocides
- create an analytical essay that compares and contrasts two genocides.

Starter
Ask pupils to study the map on pages 106–107 of *History in Progress – Book 3*, and read the surrounding caption boxes. In pairs, or as a class, pupils point out any similarities or differences between the genocides mentioned. Write down the points of comparison on the board to help with **tasks 1** and **2**.

Development

Task 1: Give pupils time to go back over the previous three enquiries before asking the class as a whole for suggestions. Suggestions could include: causes of the genocide (role of the government, propaganda, ideology, laws, poverty, civil war, historical ethnic tension, failure of external powers to act); how the genocide was carried out (centrally planned or spontaneous, industrial slaughter or primitive weapons, secret or public?) Use ideas from this list to generate further suggestions if the pupils' dry up.

Task 2: Encourage pupils to use suggestions from **task 1** to complete this task individually. They can exchange ideas afterwards. To begin, you could also ask for suggestions from some pupils in order to model the exercise for others.

Task 3: Pupils can use their table from **task 2** to structure their answer to this question. First, ask pupils to decide if, on the whole they think there were more similarities or differences between the Holocaust and the 1994 genocide in Rwanda. Then instruct pupils to start with a few paragraphs that acknowledge those areas which differ from their overall conclusion, before proceeding to make the case for their thesis. Make it clear that the pupils need to plan the order of their paragraphs to make sure they cover all their important points and stick to the question throughout.

Plenary
Select pupils to sit in a chair at the front of the class to face questions about the similarities and differences between the two genocides.

ICT opportunities
Pupils could use the internet to conduct further research into the genocides cited on the map. They could create posters or booklets about particular genocides.

> 2 Living and working

2.5 Where was life better in the 1930s: communist Russia or capitalist America?

2.5a What was life like in the USA in the 1930s?

Learning objectives
- To explore what life was like for different people in the USA in the 1930s.
- To design a poster that shows a more objective view of life in the USA.

Historical background
By 1929, America had become the world's richest nation and the leading industrial producer. This was due to huge sales revenues from the First World War, the entrepreneurialism of men such as Henry Ford pioneering new, efficient production methods, and the laissez faire attitude of the Republican governments who had ruled America since the war. However, wealth was being concentrated into fewer hands, the market was saturated with consumer goods and banks were allowed to lend money for buying shares 'on the margin'. These factors all contributed to the Wall Street Crash in October 1929, when US$30 billion were lost in a single week (over ten times the annual revenue of the American government).

Teaching Activities and Learning Outcomes

Assessment opportunity

Using sources to explore the ideas and experiences of men, women and children in past societies.

Pupils will be able to

- use evidence to explain what made people comparatively happy in 1930s America
- present their knowledge of American society in a design for a billboard poster.

Starter

Pupils look at **source a** on page 108 of *History in Progress – Book 3*. Either in pairs or in a class discussion, ask them to explain what they can see in the billboard poster and if any general conclusions can be made about American society in the 1930s from it. Ask them specifically about what 'the American Way' might mean. Have a class vote for the second question, with explanations for voting.

Development

Green task: Pupils work individually to complete this task. **Worksheet 2.5a** will help to organise their ideas into a format that can be used in the next task.

Blue task: Pupils can use **Worksheet 2.5a**. If time allows, break the class into groups of six and assign everyone a character from the sources to argue about their plight. They can then arrange themselves in a happy-sad line before proceeding with the written task. For part **b**, encourage pupils to compare the reasons that made people happy or sad.

Orange task: Pupils either describe what their poster will look like, or begin to design and make one. This could be set as homework.

Plenary

Pupils can present their ideas for their poster and receive feedback from their peers.

Cross-curricular links

Citizenship: The role of government in people's welfare, and the fairness of a rich-poor divide.

PSHE: The relationship between wealth and happiness in life.

ICT opportunities

History in Progress – LiveText CD 3: electronic activity.
Pupils could be encouraged to use the internet to research typical images of 1930s America.

2.5 Where was life better in the 1930s: communist Russia or capitalist America?

Worksheet 2.5a What was life like in the USA in the 1930s?

1 Read through **sources b–g** on page 109 of *History in Progress – Book 3*. For each source pick out details that suggest that this person was happy or sad in 1930s America and add them to the table below.

2a When you have done this, rank the sources, with 1 for the happiest and 6 for the most unhappy.

Source	Details that show person is happy:	Details that show person is unhappy:	Rank
b			
c			
d			
e			
f			
g			

2b Compare the things that made people happy or unhappy in 1930s America. What do these sources tell us about common reasons for happiness / unhappiness in 1930s America?

_____
_____
_____
_____
_____
_____

2 Living and working

2.5 Where was life better in the 1930s: communist Russia or capitalist America?

2.5b What was life like in the USSR in the 1930s?

Learning objectives
- To explore what life was like for people in Russia in the 1930s.
- To compare and contrast people's memories with contemporary sources.

Historical background

The Communist Manifesto was published on 21 February 1848, by Karl Marx, and another German philosopher, Friedrich Engels. Marx moved to London in 1849, and lived there until his death in 1883. The book inspired socialist movements across Europe, including the Russian Social Democrat Party, formed in 1889. However Lenin effectively split the Party in 1902, with his pamphlet 'What is to be Done?'. He argued against the orthodox Marxist view that Russia would have wait for a capitalist order to mature before a socialist revolution could happen; Lenin called for a small, professional group of revolutionaries to act as a vanguard for socialism. His Bolshevik ('majority') faction went on to lead the October Revolution in 1917, and, after a brutal civil war from 1918–21, form the Union of Soviet (council) Socialist Republics.

Teaching Activities and Learning Outcomes

Assessment opportunity

Evaluating and comparing sources to explore the ideas and experiences of people in past societies.

Pupils will be able to

- compare and contrast the content and provenance of a range of sources
- explain what makes one source more useful or reliable to a historian than another.

Starter

Remind pupils of the starter from the previous lesson about the fairness of having very rich and very poor people in society. As a whole class, discuss each of Marx's ideas in turn; you could ask pupils to do this in pairs first. Pupils can then rank from one to five which ones they agree with most..

Development

Green task: Pupils could do this individually or in pairs. They could use **Worksheet 2.5b (1)** to structure their research if necessary.

Blue task: Again, this can be done individually or in pairs, with the assistance of the worksheet if needed. Emphasise the need to consider the origin of the source. You could model an evaluation of one source with the class as a whole before they tackle the rest of the task.

Orange task: Ask the pupils to set out a letter in the correct fashion before they begin. Alternatively they could use **Worksheet 2.5b (2)**. The pupils should use their research from the first two tasks to complete the letter. Emphasise the need to discuss origin and reliability for part **a**, and the usefulness of source content in part **b**.

Plenary

Back to the start: Hold a class vote, or ask the pupils to vote with their feet by moving to different sides of the classroom. Ask pupils to justify where they stand on the issue.

Cross-curricular links

Citizenship: How far should citizens believe the messages of their government or the media?

2 Living and working

2.5 Where was life better in the 1930s: communist Russia or capitalist America?

Worksheet 2.5b (1) What was life like in the USSR in the 1930s?

1a Look at **source b** below (and on page 111 of *History in Progress – Book 3*). Underline, or draw arrows to bits of information that tell us about life under Stalin.

> Life under Stalin was more peaceful and happy. We were all poor, but we had lots of fun. Families shared everything they had. Today every family lives only for itself. We believed that life would get better if we worked hard. We took more pride in our work than we do today.

b

1b Now look at **sources c–g** on page 111 of *History in Progress – Book 3*. Decide whether the information in these sources support or go against Iraida's memories of life under Stalin.

Source	Points that support Iraida's memories	Points that go against Iraida's memories	Order of reliability	Points that explain the reliability of the source
b				
c				
d				
e				
f				
g				

2 Now complete the table by putting the sources in order of reliability, where 1 is the most reliable and 6 is the least reliable. Think carefully as you need to explain your order with points in the last column.

© Pearson Education Ltd 2009: History in Progress – Planning and Resource Pack 3

2 Living and working

2.5 Where was life better in the 1930s: communist Russia or capitalist America?

Worksheet 2.5b (2) What was life like in the USSR in the 1930s?

3 Complete this letter to the historian Orlando Figes.

- In your first paragraph, explain how far you think people's memories are a useful way for finding out what life was like in 1930s Russia.
- In your second paragraph explain which source gave the most useful evidence for what life was really like in 1930s Russia.
- Refer back to your notes on **task 1** and **2** to help plan and provide details for the letter.

_____ (your name)
_____ (your house and street)
_____ (your town)
_____ (your postcode)

(today's date)

Dear Mr. Figes,

My name is _____, a History student at _____.
I have recently heard that you plan to bring out a new edition of your book about life in Russia in the 1930s called The Whisperers. The first edition used a lot of people's memories ~~from the 1930s~~ to explain what life ~~was like for Russians who~~ lived back then. I would like you to consider my following points about people's memories, and other sources I have seen about Russia in the 1930s, before you write the second edition.

Overall, people's memories are a...

In addition to people's memories, you should think about using some other sources. One of the best sources I have seen is...

Yours faithfully,

2.6 How did Chairman Mao change China?

2.6a What was the Great Leap Forward?

Learning objectives
- To discover what life was like in China under Chairman Mao.
- To use sources to identify the key features of a different society.

Historical background

From 1644 to 1911, China was ruled by the Qing (pronounced 'Ching') Dynasty which retained many traditional elements of government. However, largely due to Western encroachment, there was great pressure for modernisation from students and the military. The last Qing Emperor was overthrown by a revolution in 1911; rule over China was divided among war lords. The struggle between Chiang Kai-Shek's Koumintang (KMT), and the Chinese Communist Party (CCP) turned into armed conflict. During the Long March to escape the KMT in 1934, Mao Zedong emerged as leader of the CCP. Fighting continued under Japanese occupation, and was finally resolved when Mao proclaimed the People's Republic of China on 1 October 1949.

Teaching Activities and Learning Outcomes

Assessment opportunity

Exploring the diverse experiences, ideas and beliefs of people in past societies; identifying and explaining change and continuity in China under Chairman Mao; communicating knowledge of history in a variety of ways using correct chronology and historical vocabulary.

Pupils will be able to

- explain how Mao wanted to change traditional Chinese society
- write a script for a film that shows how Mao's reforms affected ordinary people in China.

Starter

Working in pairs, pupils look at **source a** on page 112 of *History in Progress – Book 3*. Ask them to consider what types of people are shown, what they are holding, what they are attacking and what the Chinese slogan might say ('Everybody get to work to destroy the four pests'). Who would have made such a poster and why?

Development

Green task: Pupils work individually. You could begin as a class: the sources are read aloud and pupils put their hands up if they hear something to help answer the question. Pupils then write individually.

Blue task: The pupils repeat the underlining / arrow drawing of the previous task. This time, encourage the pupils to look for points of comparison between **sources c–e** before they answer the question.

Orange task: Use **Worksheet 2.6a** to help pupils prepare for this task.

Plenary

Pupils can either quiz each other about their ideas for their plot line, explaining how the family learn about the Great Leap Forward and how it affects them, or they can volunteer ideas to the class, or they could be hot-seated with other pupils asking questions.

Cross-curricular links

Citizenship: Exploring how a change in ruling ideology can make a difference to people's lives.

ICT opportunities

If resources are available, the pupils could act out some of the better scripts on film and edit them on a computer.

2 Living and working

2.6 How did Chairman Mao change China?

Worksheet 2.6a What was the Great Leap Forward?

- You are going to write a script for a film about the Peng family who live in Chen Village near Beijing.
- You can use the Peng family (father Xu Peng, mother Jun Ying, son Wing Hang and daughter Shinney), other villagers, and Chinese Communist Party members from Beijing as characters.
- Aim for at least three scenes: scene 1 should set the scene of life before the Great Leap Forward (the family living at home and farming their strip in the traditional way); scene 2 should explore how the Peng family find out about the new changes (e.g. gossip about a new poster in the village, or a big meeting) and what their reactions are (enthusiastic as they get to punish greedy neighbours? Reluctant as they like the traditional ways? Do they suffer as they are wealthy peasants?); scene 3 should show what happens to the Peng family as a result of the new changes. You may add other scenes, but they should all focus on the parents and the Great Leap Forwards.
- You should use lots of detail from the sources to make your script believable.
- You can use stage directions [written in brackets like these] as well as dialogue to describe the action.
- Before beginning the script, write some notes below to help plan what will happen in each scene.

Scene 1: Before the Great Leap Forward:

Scene 2: The Peng family find out about the Great Leap Forward:

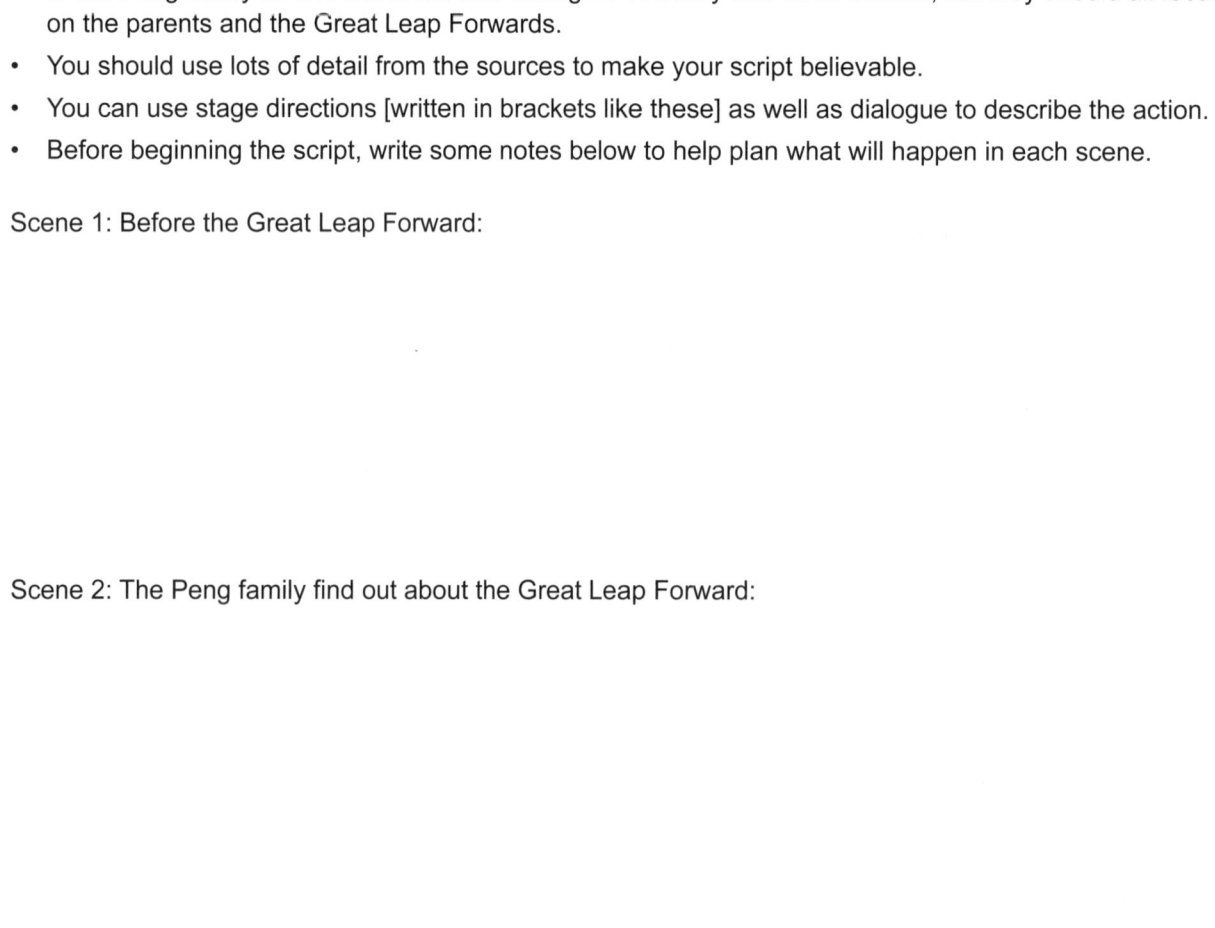

Scene 3: The new changes affect the Peng family:

2 Living and working

2.6 How did Chairman Mao change China?

2.6b What was the Cultural Revolution?

Learning objectives
- To discover what happened during the Cultural Revolution.
- To use sources to explore the effects of an event on people.

Historical background
Around 20 million people are thought to have died as a consequence of the Great Leap Forward. In 1959, Mao stood down as 'Chairman' of China in favour of Liu Shaoqi whose re-introduction of elements of the free market stabilised the situation. Mao remained Chairman of the CCP and used his influence to mount a political comeback. In 1963, he began a Socialist Education Movement to clear up 'reactionary' elements within the Party (including Liu Shaoqi). In 1965, Mao's second wife Jiang Qing (Madame Mao) began a campaign that attacked all those who opposed Mao as class traitors. It was in this context that Mao called upon the Red Guards for decisive action in 1966.

Teaching Activities and Learning Outcomes

Assessment opportunities

Exploring the diverse experiences, ideas and beliefs of people in past societies; identifying and explaining change and continuity in China under Chairman Mao; communicating knowledge of history in a variety of ways using correct chronology and historical vocabulary.

Pupils will be able to

- use sources to identify how Mao tried to change Chinese culture between 1966–69
- use sources to weigh up who was responsible for the violence in China in these years
- complete their script by showing how the Cultural Revolution affected ordinary people in China.

Starter

Pupils study **source a** (page 114 of *History in Progress – Book 3*), and come up with theories on how it was allowed to take place. Ask pupils what we might learn about the rest of society from this photo. What would it be like to live in a society where this type of behaviour was acceptable?

Development

Green task: Pupils can complete this task individually or in pairs. Model the task using **source a** on page 114 of *History in Progress – Book 3* as an example (old learning being challenged). Explain what is being changed and then use details from the source to justify the point.

Blue task: Working in pairs, pupils need to decide which source better supports the idea of Mao (leadership and guidance from above), the Red Guards (spontaneous action) or both as being to blame. They must explain using details form the source. **Worksheet 2.6b (1)** will help structure their answers.

Orange task: The pupils can now complete the script they began in the previous enquiry. Remind them that the same rules still apply about stage directions and dialogue. This time characters could include the Peng family, Red Guards, teachers and perhaps even Mao. Use **Worksheet 2.6b (2)** to prepare them.

Plenary

Back to the Start: This discussion could start with a vote; then ask pupils to justify their decisions.

Cross-curricular links

Citizenship: The role of laws and customs to preserve order in society.

ICT opportunities

If resources allow, the pupils could act out and film some of the scripts, then edit them on a computer.

2 Living and working

2.6 How did Chairman Mao change China?

Worksheet 2.6b (1) What was the Cultural Revolution?

- Look at **sources a–e** on pages 114–115 of *History in Progress – Book 3*, and use them to complete the diagram below. You must decide whether the information in the source suggests that Mao, the Red Guards or both were responsible for the violence that took place during the Cultural Revolution.
- Remember to use key pieces of information from the source to explain where you have placed it on the diagram.

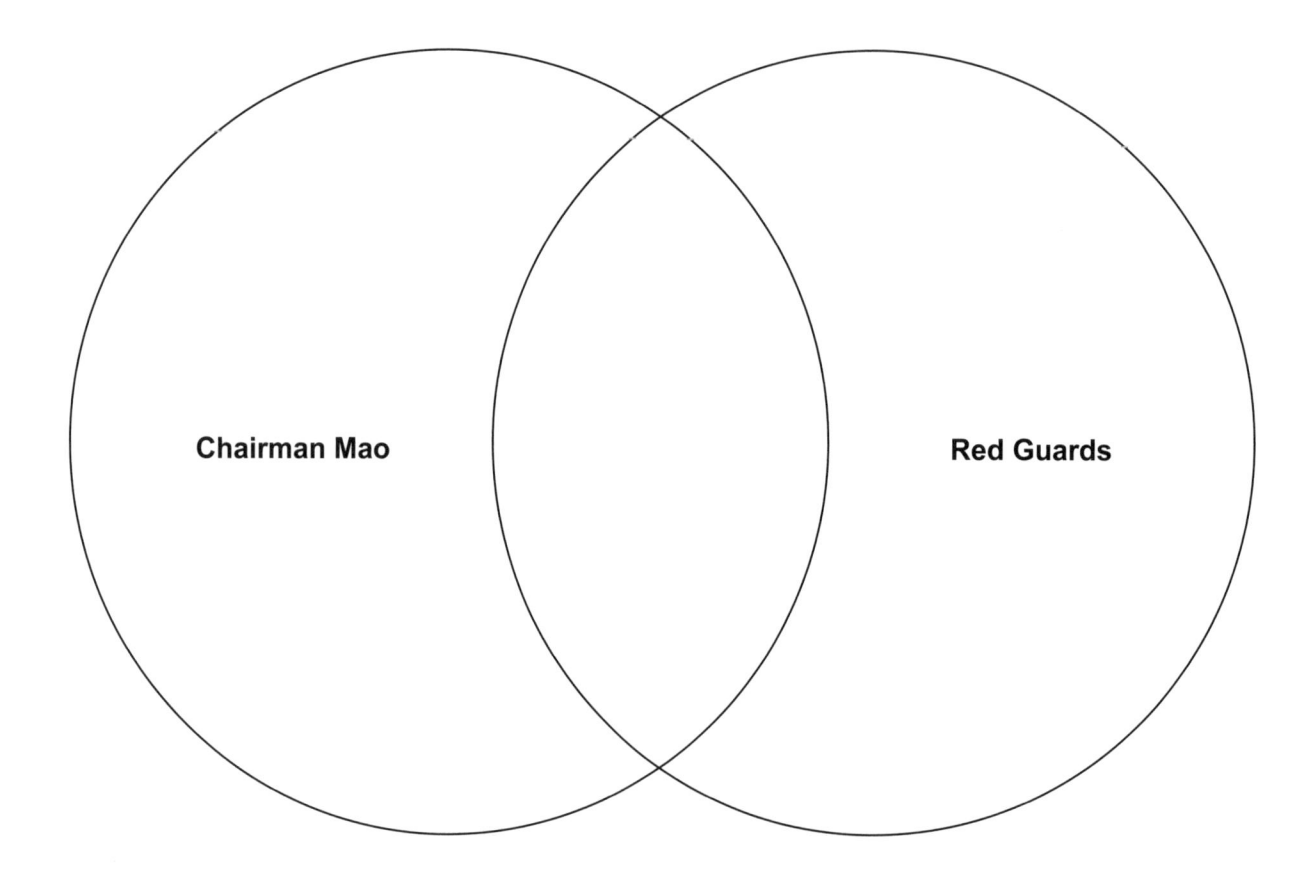

Chairman Mao | **Red Guards**

2.6 How did Chairman Mao change China?

Worksheet 2.6b (2) What was the Cultural Revolution?

- You are going to finish your script for a film about the Peng family.
- You can use the Peng family (focusing on Wing Hang and Shinney), Red Guards and perhaps Chairman Mao as characters.
- Aim for at least two scenes: scene 1 (or 4 of the whole script) should show the Peng children hearing about the Cultural Revolution; scene 2 (or 5) should explore how the children react to the new changes, especially the rise of the Red Guards. You may add other scenes, but they should all focus on the children and the Cultural Revolution.
- You should use lots of detail from the sources to make your script believable.
- You can use stage directions [written in brackets like these] as well as dialogue to describe the action.
- Before beginning the script, write some notes below to help plan what will happen in each scene.

Scene 1 (or 4): Wing Hang and Shinney hear about the Cultural Revolution:

Scene 2 (or 5): Wing Hang and Shinney decide what to do when the Red Guards are set up at school:

> 2 Living and working

2.7 Did the Cold War lead to an age of fear?

2.7a What was the Cold War?

Learning objectives
- To learn about the extent and dangers of the Cold War.
- To recognise the significance of events that contributed to the tensions during the conflict.

Historical background
With the end of the Second World War, it might have been assumed by those celebrating that the world could expect a period of peace and increasing prosperity amongst mutually friendly countries. In fact, for the next fifty years, tensions between the West and the Eastern Bloc countries, carried out in the shadow of nuclear war, created a climate of fear that encompassed the lives of ordinary people across the globe, in a way that the Second World War never had.

Teaching Activities and Learning Outcomes

Assessment opportunity

Making links as to the causes of increased international tension in the post war period.

Pupils will be able to

- identify and describe some of the key concerns that contemporary politicians held
- recognise and classify the nature of threats to the relationship between East and West
- explain how a Cold War could be seen as being more terrifying than a conventional war.

Starter

As a counter-point to the Cold War, pupils are asked to focus on the possible emotional reactions felt at the end of the Second World War. Pupils should be encouraged to think about aspects of life that would change, as well as aspirations people would have had for themselves and their children now that the war is over.

Development

Green task: Pupils should read **source b**, on page 116 of *History in Progress – Book 3*. Discuss what a curtain does; what is gained and lost by drawing one over a scene? How would an 'iron' curtain be different? Pupils then read **source a**, on page 116 of *History in Progress – Book 3*, to gain an understanding of what Churchill actually meant. Use the map, on page 117, to study locations and discuss whether drawing the curtain in a different place would have affected security of the East or West.

Blue task: Pupils use the table on page 117 of *History in Progress – Book 3* to probe their understanding and importance of events. An extension of this would be to ask pupils to rank the events according to the danger / effect they had on the developing situation.

Orange task: An alternative method of completing this task would be to divide the group into two with each group focusing on a different aspect. One side provides a discussion as to why a conventional war is more dangerous than a cold war, and vice versa. Pupils should focus on the key issue of fear.

Plenary

Ask pupils to write down three statements on the problems of living with nuclear weapons. One should be from a child, one from a parent and the third from a politician. Share the three statements across the class to judge the understanding of the issues so far.

Cross-curricular links

Geography, Citizenship

2 Living and working

2.7 Did the Cold War lead to an age of fear?

2.7b Living in the shadow of the bomb: Cuba

Learning objectives
- To learn about what happened during the Cuban Missile Crisis.
- To explain why President Kennedy made his decisions in the crisis.

Historical background

A generation after both the USA and the USSR had obtained nuclear weapons, there came a defining point in the Cold War: Soviet missiles, capable of carrying nuclear warheads to major American cities, were discovered on the island of Cuba. The discovery brought the two superpowers to the brink of nuclear war. The whole world held it's breath as President Kennedy and President Krushchev sought to resolve the issues of nuclear deployment.

Teaching Activities and Learning Outcomes

Assessment opportunity

Use of sources to evaluate a historical event.

Pupils will be able to

- recognise the significance of the location of missile deployments to the targeted countries
- highlight and construct newspaper headlines based on source evidence
- explain why President Kennedy acted in the way he did during the crisis.

Starter

On a simple level pupils might be able to recognise that Kennedy was the last to assume power, but a more complex view might reveal that there were close relationships between Cuba and the USA.

Development

Green task: In order to establish the context, pupils should be asked to consider the location of nuclear tipped missiles in relation to their distance. Using the world map (page 118 of *History in Progress – Book 3*), begin with Russia and Turkey first. Ask: 'If this was us what would our reaction be?' Follow this up by looking at the map of North America (page 119 of *History in Progress – Book 3*). Ask: 'Should the site of Soviet missiles have been a surprise to the USA and why?'

Blue task: Pupils are asked to come up with headlines that either dramatize or play down a particular event. They should consider when and why such headlines might be used by the press.

Orange task: An extension of Kennedy's diary could be to provide reasons about why he felt it was necessary to keep some material secret.

Plenary

The 'hot line' was set up between the Presidents at the end of the crisis. Ask students to make a brief list of all the other ways in which we communicate and are able to observe what is happening in the world. Could another 'Cuba' happen today? Does modern technology makes us more safe, or less?

Cross-curricular links

Geography, Media

> 2 Living and working

2.7 Did the Cold War lead to an age of fear?

2.7c How to survive a nuclear attack

Learning objectives
- To learn about how people were encouraged to treat the threats of nuclear war.
- To develop a perspective of how people saw events at the time.

Historical background
The Cold War affected everyone living in countries that were possible targets. During times of extreme tension between the superpowers – in the 1950s and 1980s especially – advice was given to the public at large, and to children, about what to expect and how to react if nuclear war started.

Teaching Activities and Learning Outcomes

Assessment opportunity

Using sources to develop empathy with people in the past.

Pupils will be able to

- recognise and understand the affect of nuclear weapons on people
- compare, contrast and explain the differences in how people were prepared for nuclear war
- explain how and why people react to the threat of nuclear war.

Starter

Ask pupils about the type of weapons that they know are used in wars, and how they are used. Are there any that should be banned and why? An alternative would be to provide descriptions of different weapons that they have come across in their studies and ask them to select only a certain number as being legal. This will force a debate as to the impact of weaponry on people. Further development can be produced by asking what weapons can be legally used on troops / civilian populations and why?

Development

Green task: Pupils could be encouraged to consider the overall effect of such a weapon by considering the problems that their own town would face if such an event happened. A local map marked with the 0.5km and 35km boundaries could be given out and pupils asked to consider how the town would cope today. What would be the biggest problems and why?

Blue task: The advice given to people in the 1950s and 1980s does have some differences; pupils should identify these, and then be asked what advice they think would be given to people today, and what the effect would be.

Orange task: This could be completed initially as a spider diagram to collect their thoughts before developing the explanation.

Plenary

Use a simple thumb up / down / middle as a response to the statement / question. Ask pupils to work in pairs to discuss how much of a threat (on a scale of one to ten) they feel they are under at the moment. Take feedback from one of the pair asking them to explain why they think their decision is correct.

Cross-curricular links

Media, Citizenship, Science

2.7 Did the Cold War lead to an age of fear?

2.7d Life behind the wall

Learning objectives
- To understand how people felt about the fall of the Berlin Wall.
- To use sources to establish a point of view.

Historical background
Nothing came to symbolise the Cold War as much as the building of the Berlin Wall in 1961. This was Churchill's 'Iron Curtain' made real. The different ways of life for ordinary citizens in the democratic West and the communist East was thrown into stark relief. Only with the collapse of the East German regime in 1989, and the subsequent removal of the wall, to many an icon of oppression, did the Cold War itself end.

Teaching Activities and Learning Outcomes

Assessment opportunity

Using source material to provide an assessment of an historical period.

Pupils will be able to

- identify the consequences of the construction of the wall for the people of Berlin
- describe what life was like for people who lived in East Berlin
- reach a conclusion as to the importance of the destruction of the Berlin wall.

Starter

The starter probes how people feel about being separated from loved ones. This could be completed in pairs using spider diagrams, or making a list of possible emotional effects. This should then be developed into asking whether there is ever a reason for dividing people up in this way, and if so when?

Development

Green task: The response to this task may overlap the starter, but the focus should be to enable pupils to consider the affect on ordinary people of having a population torn in two. Pupils could be provided with examples of institutions and communities that have been split (schools, hospitals, transport etc.) and asked to consider where the greatest impact may be.

Blue task: Ask pupils to divide an A4 piece of paper into two by drawing an image of a wall. One side should be labelled 'advantages' and the other, 'disadvantages.' Pupils should then write the advantages of living in East Berlin on one side and the disadvantages on the other. Ask the class to think of a keyword that describes their impression of living in East Berlin. Is this the same for everyone?

Orange task: Pupils are asked to consider whether the Berlin Wall was an icon of the period, and what its significance is. Does the fact that some surviving pieces of the wall are held in museums across the globe (e.g. the Imperial War Museum in London) support their view and why?

Plenary

Are there any other examples of walls being built to separate societies? Show images of Northern Ireland and Israel. Find out what pupils know about these walls and probe their understanding of the reasons for building walls as a means of maintaining a way of life.

Cross-curricular links

Geography, Media

> 2 Living and working

2.8 How did healthcare change in the twentieth century?

2.8a Which was the greatest breakthrough in healthcare?

Learning objectives
- To learn about the impact of individuals in changes in healthcare.
- To develop and apply criteria in order to reach a conclusion.

Historical background
The twentieth century was a remarkable time for the development of medicine and the understanding of the workings of the human body. Such advances were the result of years of labour, and also the inspiration of individuals who were able to unlock new ways of seeing old problems. The contribution of these individuals has brought about profound changes to the way we live now and will live in the future.

Teaching Activities and Learning Outcomes

Assessment opportunity

Evaluation of the significance of an individual achievements within a historical context.

Pupils will be able to

- recognise and relate the importance of an event within a historical context
- explain the importance of a historical individual's work
- develop appropriate criteria to reach a conclusion

Starter

Provide pupils with a set of cards [**Worksheet 2.8a (1)**] on which are a range of significant and not-so-significant medical advances, some are left blank for their own thoughts. Students can then use the cards to produce a list that they then need to justify to a partner or wider group.

Development

Green task: Task 2 should be completed in pairs. Prompt pupils to think about questions that would provide readers with information they might want. They should share their two best questions with the class. **Worksheet 2.8a (2)** will help focus pupils on the impact of the individuals.

Blue task: To extend this exercise, ask four volunteers to come to the front to represent each of the individuals. Based on their own choice in the written exercise, pupils vote for who is the most important / significant individual. Based on the voting patterns of the class ask whether anyone wants to change their individual views and why?

Orange task: A key aspect of this exercise is to establish defendable criteria. Providing possible criteria for students in the first instance, before asking them to come up with one other, can support students not used to creating and developing criteria. Collecting the suggestions together, after a class discussion, and allowing them to select from a list, provides the opportunity for students to produce work based on their own understanding and knowledge. As an alternative to 100 words a short three-slide PowerPoint could be employed.

Plenary

Use the counterfactual technique of asking / listing how different the world would be without the discoveries of the four pioneers. Ask one student to give a response before 'bouncing' the answer around the room. Asking other students to build and develop the answer will reveal the depth of understanding of the topic.

Cross-curricular links

Science, Media, Citizenship

2.8 How did healthcare change in the twentieth century?

Worksheet 2.8a (1) Which was the greatest breakthrough in healthcare?

There were many medical breakthroughs in the twentieth century but which do you think was the most significant?

Use the cards below to make a rank order as to how significant they were. Some have been left blank to let you put in your own ideas.

The discovery of stem cells		Blood transfusions	Anti smoking campaigns
Clean Air laws	Discovery of DNA		Plastic surgery
The NHS		Transplant technology	
Mass vaccinations	Key hole surgery	Better housing	X-Rays
Whole body scanning	Diet and exercise	Penicillin	
Dental services	The female contraceptive pill		Providing school meals

How would you re-order your cards if you were asked to think about the impact on the following groups of people:

Children

The elderly

Women

Men

2 Living and working

2.8 How did healthcare change in the twentieth century?

Worksheet 2.8a (2) Which was the greatest breakthrough in healthcare?

2 Look at the fact files below. How would you rate each of the characters in the four categories? Use the tables on each factfile below to help you make your judgements.

Achievement: Measure of how 'groundbreaking' their discoveries were.
Recognition: the extent to which their fellow scientists officially recognised the importance of their work.
Fame: How well recognised they were by scientists and media alike.
Impact: The extent to which their methods have improved life for people.

Facfile 1

Christiaan Barnard, 1922–2001

Nobel Prize: None

Area of research: Transplant surgery

Background: Barnard was a highly respected surgeon who developed the techniques he used by experimenting on animals hearts without lasting success. However in 1967, he successfully transplanted a human heart to man suffering incurable heart disease. He became an overnight superstar with the world media for his achievements.

Legacy: Today transplant surgery of all types is a routine way of extending people's lives.

Achievement				
Recognition				
Fame				
Impact				

Facfile 2

Marie Curie, 1867–1934

Nobel Prize: Physics 1903 and Chemistry 1911

Area of research: Development of X-Rays

Background: Recognised as a pioneer in her field, Marie Curie's research was crucial in the development of x-rays in surgery. She discovered and was able to use radioactive radium to reduce suffering amongst patients and equipped ambulances with x-ray machines were used on the front lines During World War One. Later she received many honorary science medicine and law degrees for her work.

Legacy: Today X-Rays are widely used in the treatment of cancers and are used to 'see' inside the body.

Achievement				
Recognition				
Fame				
Impact				

Facfile 3

Alexander Fleming, 1881–1955

Nobel Prize: Medicine 1945

Area of research: Bacteriology

Background: In 1928, while conducting an experiment, Fleming discovered that a mould that had accidentally infected a culture dish growing skin disease germs had created a bacteria-free circle around itself that killed the germs. After more experiments Fleming named the active substance penicillin. His discovery brought him a wide range of honours.

Legacy: Today penicillin is widely used to combat bacterial infections and disease around the world.

Achievement				
Recognition				
Fame				
Impact				

Facfile 4

James Watson 1928–
Francis Crick 1916–2004

Nobel Prize: Medicine 1962

Area of research: DNA

Background: In 1951, the two Cambridge scientists began work on trying to understand how the body is able to recreate its self and how human genes transmit their information to the next generation. In 1953 they were able to explain to the world how DNA works. Since then they have received many honours in recognition of one of the discoveries of the 20th century.

Legacy: The ability to understand DNA works has helped in the development of better drugs to understand and develop cures for a range of diseases and has revolutionised forensic science.

Achievement				
Recognition				
Fame				
Impact				

2.8 How did healthcare change in the twentieth century?

2.8b Out with the old; in with the new

Learning objectives
- To learn about the impact of the National Health Service on people's health.
- To assess the value of the National Health Service.

Historical background
The National Health Service (NHS) in Britain, with its 'free treatment at the point of need' has made a major contribution to the improvement in the quality of life for many Britons for the last half century. The core of the provision is the way in which it is funded. With an aging population and increasing needs, this unit questions the way that money is raised and whether there are acceptable alternatives.

Teaching Activities and Learning Outcomes

Assessment opportunity

Evaluating the strength and depth of opposing viewpoints.

Pupils will be able to

- state an opinion about the nature of changes to health care over time
- describe and explain the advantages of the NHS in a historical context
- develop a valid argument on the appropriate provision of healthcare in Britain.

Starter

A spider diagram is the most appropriate way to get the ideas down for this exercise. Ask pupils to do this in pairs, and then circulate the completed diagrams around the room for pupils to add additional items as appropriate. Ask the class to what extent they were aware of the many different ways the health service provides support, and which surprise them. Save the diagrams for the plenary.

Development

Green task: In asking pupils to complete this simple exercise the focus should be on inference: 'If these are the sources we know about, what more might we conclude is true?' This will open a discussion in which pupils' understanding of the health service can be explored.

Blue task: It is important to identify what pupils already know about the American health service before starting this task. An opening question to probe this could focus on what life might be like in Britain if we all had to have health insurance. From a deeper understanding of the context, the actual question should be used alongside the table to produce an answer.

Orange task: Developing a balanced opinion may be problematical for some pupils, therefore asking pupils to produce a small booklet identifying advantages and disadvantages of each system is a way of allowing them to rehearse the arguments before completing the final work.

Plenary

Return to the spider diagrams used at the start. To explore the pupils' understanding of the significance of the NHS, pose the following question: 'The health service has only so much money – which of these services do you consider essential and why?' Pupils mark these onto their diagrams and justify either through discussion or in a written format.

Cross-curricular links

Science: Advances to healthcare

Citizenship: Access to healthcare

> 2 Living and working

2.9 What was it like 'back in my day …'?

2.9a You've never had it so good: Britain in the 1950s

Learning objectives
- To investigate the influences on young people in Britain growing up in the 1950s.
- To use sources to reach conclusions about a historical period.

Historical background
At the beginning of the 1950s, people were still suffering the aftermath and privations of the Second World War. By the end of the decade, the Prime Minister was voicing the misquoted opinion that: 'You've never had it so good' to the press. Children growing up in the 1950s lived in a country that rejoiced in great achievements, while at the same time struggled with increasing social change.

Teaching Activities and Learning Outcomes

Assessment opportunity

Selecting and using evidence to challenge a contemporary interpretation of the past.

Pupils will be able to

- understand and describe the emotions of children in a contemporary setting
- select and explain how historical sources support a particular interpretation of the past
- determine and explain the validity of differing views of a contemporary period.

Starter

In order to provide the context of a 'scrapbook' pupils are asked to consider key moments from their own life so far. *Handle this with care*, perhaps ask the class to focus on specific issues that have resulted in a happy or shared memory. Ask pupils to rank their answers in order to identify a key issue which can be compared with others in the class.

Development

Green task: Working individually, pupils come up with a list of words that they feel describes the sensations of the children involved. The second part of the task should be done as a whole class discussion to pick up on differences through the group.

Blue task: Pupils are asked to prepare their questions before embarking on the interview. You could either make groups of three (with one of the three as Mel), or take the 'hot seat' yourself. Pupils make a note of the answers and use these notes to write a conclusion that can contribute to a discussion or a short piece of writing.

Orange task: Pupils could debate the three statements in groups, or this could be a written exercise with pupils encouraged to provide reasons for dismissing two of the statements, as well as justifying their final choice.

Plenary

Ask pupils to rank **sources a–h** (pages 130–131 of *History in Progress – Book 3*) in terms of importance from the point of view of a child living at the time, and then an adult. What reasons can they identify as to why lists amongst the class might be different?

Cross-curricular links

Citizenship

2.9 What was it like 'back in my day ...'?

2.9b Growing up in the 1960s

Learning objectives
- To learn about key moments in the life of a person living in the 1960s.
- To evaluate the motivation and purpose of collecting historical sources.

Historical background
If the 1950s had seemed like a time of change to children growing up in Britain, it was nothing compared to the 1960s. Throughout the decade advancements in communications, technology and medicine overturned social norms that had lasted for generations. It was a time to be young. Nevertheless, not everyone found the pace of change to their tastes, and the decade was to witness several 'dark' moments before it was over.

Teaching Activities and Learning Outcomes

Assessment opportunity

Classifying and evaluating source material to produce an interpretation of the past.

Pupils will be able to

- group sources into relevant categories
- justify selections of sources in terms of historical importance
- determine to what extent a period of time can be summarised by key features or characteristics.

Starter

Build on the last lesson by encouraging pupils to consider what might be key moments for them between the ages they are now and turning thirty. There are some obvious answers so, to extend and develop the exercise, different topical areas might be suggested (i.e. sport events, joint ventures). Compare timelines throughout the class to highlight the pupils' values. This can be used later for the orange task.

Development

Green task: Pupils are asked to group source materials together according to their own views. An extension of this task would be to provide three or four category headings. Include an ambiguous one like 'challenge' in order to probe the pupils' understanding of the sources.

Blue task: Pupils are asked to work individually to rank **sources a–h** (pages 132–133 of *History in Progress – Book 3*) in order of importance. Answers are then 'snowballed' (first pairs, then fours, then eights etc.) in order to reach a degree of consensus.

Orange task: Pupils are asked to categorise the 1960s in 100 words by selecting a single term. The importance here is their ability to justify the word that they chose. A development of the exercise is to allow pupils either to have a smaller list of words (in which case some of the sources would not fit) or a longer list. Pupils could also research the period further to find additional sources to support a given title.

Plenary

Ask pupils to consider the last few years. If they were constructing a scrap book today, what word would they put on the front of the book and why?

Cross-curricular links

Citizenship

> 2 Living and working

2.10 What role did trade unions play in people's lives?

2.10a Why join a union?

Learning objectives
- To find out what trade unions are, and how they have tried to improve things for workers.
- To use a case study to make general conclusions about a historical issue.

Historical background

Trade unions (or 'combinations') began to form at the end of the eighteenth century. In 1871, with the passing of the Trade Union Act, they gained legal status. The 1906 Trades Dispute Act meant that unions could not be sued for loss of profit caused by a strike. The 1913 Trade Union Act allowed unions to fund political parties with an opt-out clause for members. This set up lasted until the Trade Union Act of 1927 when an opt-in clause was restored; this Act was in response to the General Strike of 1926, and made general or sympathetic strikes illegal. Trade unions weakened in the 1930s due to the scale of unemployment but, as in the First World War, grew stronger in the full employment of the war years.

Teaching Activities and Learning Outcomes

Assessment opportunity

Developing a chronological understanding of a period by exploring a key feature of British society; considering the significance of trade unions in their historical context.

Pupils will be able to

- extract relevant information from a narrative source and decide how far it can be used to support a general conclusion
- consider the strengths and limitations of a narrow case study in a broad historical enquiry.

Starter

Pupils could tackle this question in pairs or in a group. Encourage them to think of at least two different suggestions. These can then be shared with the class. Ask the pupils to reflect on the merits and limitations of various suggestions.

Development

Green task: Pupils should work individually on this task. They could use **Worksheet 2.10a** to organise their research.

Blue task: This could be done individually or in pairs. **Worksheet 2.10a** encourages pupils to move onto this question when they have finished the previous task.

Orange task: Pupils could answer this as a written exercise with two paragraphs (one on strengths / use, one on limits). It could also be done as a group discussion, perhaps before setting the written task.

Plenary

Discuss how realistic a pupils' union would be at the school. What methods could be used? What could be achieved that workers' trade unions have achieved? What problems might be faced? Look ahead to the next enquiry by asking what would happen if a very forceful leader tried to break the power of the unions, and if anyone knows someone who is / was in a trade union.

Cross-curricular links

Citizenship: Exploring the role of non-governmental organisations in society.

2.10 What role did trade unions play in people's lives?

Worksheet 2.10a Why join a union?

1 Read through the conversation between Arthur, Michael and Christopher on page 135 of *History in Progress – Book 3*. Use the information in the speech bubbles to complete the timeline below. Next to each date, explain the significance of that year to the Jenkins family.

2a Decide whether the information for that year shows whether:

- trade unions helped the Jenkins family
- trade unions did not help the Jenkins family
- it does not tell us anything about whether trade unions helped the Jenkins family.

Year	Significance of that year to the family?	Does this show that trade unions helped the family?
1904		
1908		
1912		
1914–18		
1921		
1925		
1926		
1931		
1945		
1950		

> 2 Living and working

2.10 What role did trade unions play in people's lives?

2.10b Why did miners strike?

Learning objectives
- To explore the impact of the 1984 miners' strike on ordinary people.
- To prepare to carry out some local oral history about life in the 1980s.

Historical background
Since 1947 the coal industry had been run by the National Coal Board (NCB), with large subsidies from the government. In 1983, Ian MacGregor was appointed by the Conservative Prime Minister, Margaret Thatcher, to run the NCB. He announced the closure of twenty pits, with the loss of 20,000 jobs. Arthur Scargill, leader of the National Union of Miners (NUM) encouraged regional branches to organise strikes without holding a national secret ballot on strike action. The NUM was fined; strikers were not entitled to benefits and police were used on several occasions. In March 1985, due to large coal stockpiles and a lack of support from other unions, the strike was finally defeated. The coal industry was privatised in 1994 and the number of active pits has fallen to a mere handful.

Teaching Activities and Learning Outcomes

Homework

Using questions devised in class, pupils conduct an interview with a relative, family friend or a teacher about trade unions and then write a report based on their interview.

Pupils will be able to

- frame an enquiry using suitable questions
- carry out some local oral history and reflect on how useful this was to find out about the recent past.

Starter

Pupils could be set a target of three different words or phrases to describe Thatcher. Their suggestions could be written on the board with positive words on one side and negative words on the other side.

Development

Green task: Discuss things pupils might be able to find out about the recent past by interviewing people who lived through those years. Write suggested categories on the board as a prompt.

Blue task: Task 2a could be done individually or in pairs. **Worksheet 2.10b** will help structure research. **Task 2b** should be done individually; ask pupils to volunteer some questions to model the task for their peers.

Orange task: Pupils choose an author from **sources b–f** on pages 136–137 of *History in Progress – Book 3* and take it in turns to interview each other. Pupils should use information in the sources when answering questions about the strike. They should practice taking notes to write a report from.

Plenary

Debate the question: 'How popular or successful do you think trade unions have been in twentieth century Britain?' Encourage pupils to refer back to the previous enquiry. Finish with a class vote.

Cross-curricular links

Citizenship: Non-governmental organisations in society.

PSHE: Using recent history to discover identity.

ICT opportunities

Pupils could use the internet to carry out further research about trade unions or the 1980s.

2.10 What role did trade unions play in people's lives?

Worksheet 2.10b Why did miners strike?

2a Look at **sources b–f** on pages 136–137 of *History in Progress – Book 3*.

- Use the information in the sources to decide whether it suggests the miners' strike was popular or not
- Use the origin of the source to decide whether the source is a reliable guide to the popularity of the miners' strike.

source	The strike: popular or unpopular?	Information that shows this:	The source: reliable?	Explain your answer:
b				
c				
d				
e				
f				

© Pearson Education Ltd 2009: History in Progress – Planning and Resource Pack 3

Unit 2 Living and Working

2.11 Making connections: Twentieth century Exhibition

Learning objectives
- To understand that events can have both positive and negative impacts.
- To select items for relevance to an enquiry.

Teaching Activities and Learning Outcomes

Assessment opportunity

The main thrust of this lesson lies in selection and deployment for a specific purpose. All the tasks provide an assessment opportunity for these particular skills. However, this task has been designed for group work. Any assessment should take account of this and individual pupils' contributions must be able to be identified.

Starter

As a class, look at the images on page 138–139 of *History in Progress – Book 3*, and generate a list of positives and negatives from them. Try to get at least one negative from a positive-looking image and at least one positive from a negative-looking image.

Development

Green task: Pupils may need some help with starting to select positive and negatives from the student book and if time presses, this could be taken as a whole class plenary.

Blue task: Encourage discussion and the sharing of ideas. If possible, provide each group with a display board, a large sheet of paper and/or access to a computer.

Orange task: Criticising the work of others is a tricky task at the best of times. Emphasise the need to be positive in finding things to praise and that anything negative should always be supported by alternative suggestions. Aim to get over the concept of constructive criticism.

NB. These tasks will take time if they are done thoroughly and pupils become absorbed. If time is short, it has been suggested that the green task is taken as a whole class plenary. Ideally, this Making Connections section should be spread over two lessons.

Plenary

Presentation of an exhibition and its associated criticism. Does everyone agree?

Cross-curricular links

English

ICT opportunities

Creating an exhibition; writing up a critique of an exhibition.

Unit 2 Living and working

Assessment Unit 2

2.12 Assessment task 1: Was it a better to be a child in 1918, 1955 or 2005?

Pupils will be able to

- compare and contrast key features across three time periods
- identify and explain how the significance of an event differs according to viewpoint of a person.

What the task is about

- The task asks pupils to compare the viewpoints of three periods of history, and to identify and evaluate key features in order to reach a conclusion.
- Pupils are asked to think about three key time periods individually using evidence that they have collected from the unit. They focus on how a child in 1918, 1955 and 2000 would perceive the world that they live in. **Worksheet 2.12 (1)** will help.
- When addressing the four areas of **task 1** (page 140 of *History in Progress – Book 3*), answering in the first person would be an appropriate mechanism to achieve the answers. The age of the child should be similar to the age of the pupil completing the assessment.
- With the Venn diagram [**Worksheet 2.12 (2)**], pupils should use the answers from the first exercise to share their thoughts with a partner or partners. Paired discussion is key; teacher questioning should focus on whether there are alternative answers, rather than confirming that something is right or wrong.
- With the final question, working through the 'How might you complete this letter?' outline before beginning the task will provide pupils with 'stepping stones' against which they can self-evaluate their own answers. **Worksheet 2.12 (3)** will help them with this.
- An extension of the assessment would be to ask pupils to consider how a child of today might respond.

2.13 Assessment task 2: What was life like in the twentieth century?

Pupils will be able to

- interpret information as part of an enquiry into life in the twentieth century.

What the task is about

- The initial focus for students is to consider each of the sources separately to enable a structured approach to the overall task. A first step would be to use an inference 'square' (**Worksheet 2.13**) for each source. This allows pupils to place key words and ideas within a separate frame for each of numbered questions.
- The assessment might be completed initially in a group of five. If so, each pupil should complete an inference square for one source, and then the sheets should be circulated around the class for other students to add to. Corrections or errors need to be initialled by the student making them.
- The collected evidence will then need to be discussed in the group, such as issues arising from the sources (why they were produced, by whom, the nature of the source, secondary or primary etc.) before individually completing the written task.
- Additional challenge can be created by asking students to consider how interpretations might differ if the number or type of sources were restricted.

2 Living and working

Unit 2 Assessment 1

Worksheet 2.12 (1) Was it a better to be a child in 1918, 1955 or 2005?

Imagine that three children, one from 1918, one from 1955 and one from 2005, could meet together to talk about the world in which they live in. For each child use the thought bubbles to identify key words that describe their era.

2005

- I am proud to live now because…
- I think my country is important because…
- Things that have changed recently are…
- The things that pose a danger to the way I live are…

1955

- I am proud to live now because…
- I think my country is important because…
- Things that have changed recently are…
- The things that pose a danger to the way I live are…

1918

- I am proud to live now because…
- I think my country is important because…
- Things that have changed recently are…
- The things that pose a danger to the way I live are…

122 © Pearson Education Ltd 2009: History in Progress – Planning and Resource Pack 3

2 Living and working

Unit 2 Assessment 1

Worksheet 2.12 (2) Was it a better to be a child in 1918, 1955 or 2005?

With a partner use your answers from the spider diagram to add words to the Venn diagram below. Where you feel the same word can be used for two or more of the children place that word in the overlapping sections. For each word that you place, explain to your partner the reason why you have located it in that section of the diagram.

Compare your answers with two other groups from your class.

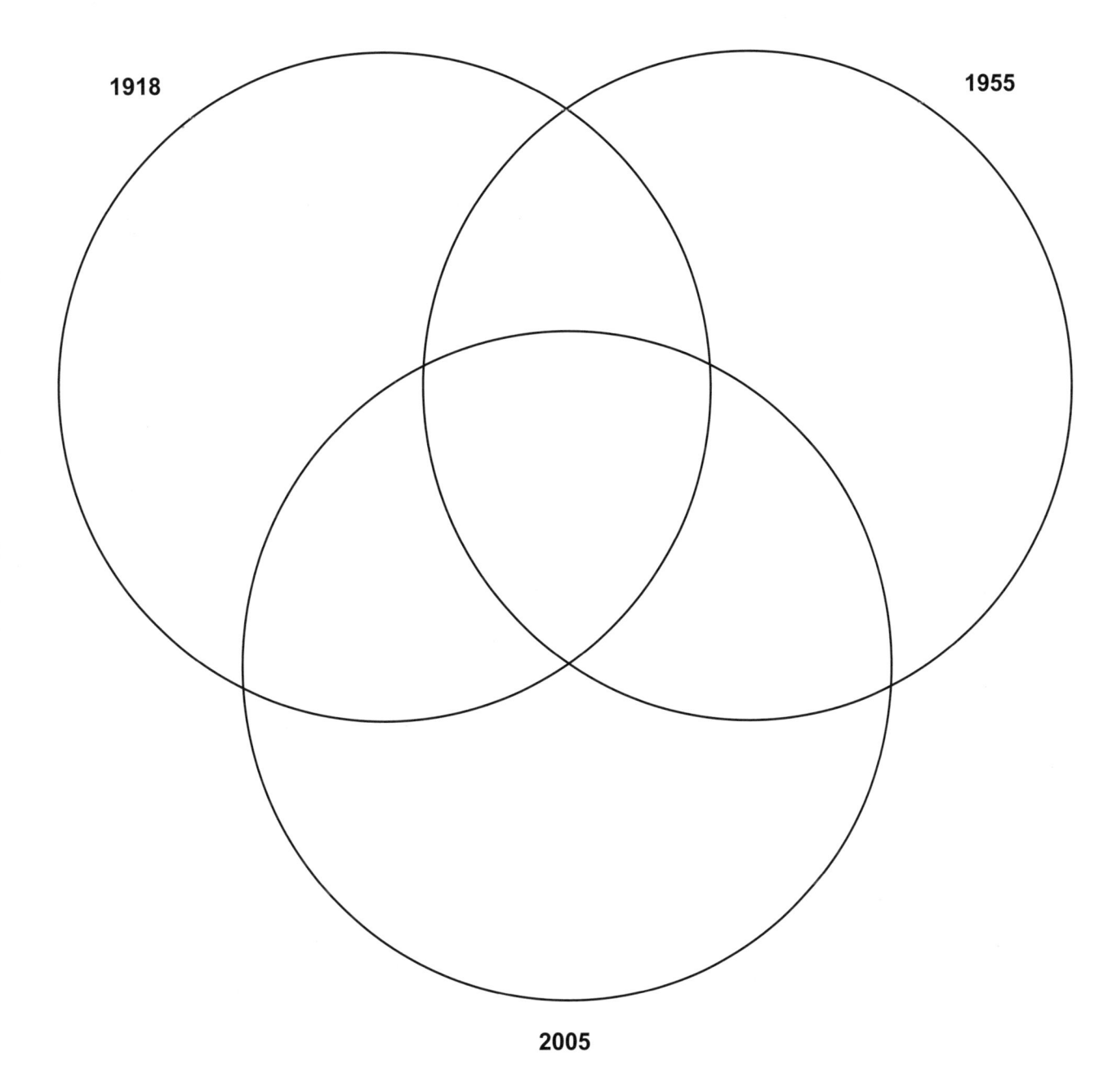

1918　　　　　　　　　　　　　　　　　　　　　　**1955**

2005

© Pearson Education Ltd 2009: History in Progress – Planning and Resource Pack 3

> 2 Living and working

Unit 2 Assessment 1

Worksheet 2.12 (3) Was it better to be a child in 1918, 1955 or 2005?

How did you do?

Level 5: I was able to …

describe some of the main features of the period	
recognise and describe how some things have changed while others have stayed the same	
suggest a relationship between causes	
produce structured work.	

Level 6: I was able to …

explain the type of change and continuity (how things stayed the same) and how these changed	
begin to explain relationships between causes	
select, organise and use information, including the correct historical words, to produce structured work.	

Level 7: I was able to …

explain how change and continuity differed over time and between places and peoples	
begin to explain why the significance of events, people and changes differed according to different viewpoints.	
Select, organise, and use the right information and the correct historical words to produce well-structured work.	

Things I did well: _____

_____

I need to learn more about: _____

One thing I could do to improve is: _____

_____

I will do this by: _____

Pupil comment: _____

_____

_____

Teacher comment: _____

_____

Unit 2 Assessment 2

Worksheet 2.13 (1) What was life like in the twentieth century?

You have been asked to write an article for a new publication, 'The Young Historian'. The audience for the new magazine are students between the ages of eleven and fourteen. For the first issue the editor wants to focus on explaining what life was like in the twentieth century.

You will be given some sources **a-e** to look at, and a strict word limit of 300 words.

Before you start, select one of the sources that you have been given. Place it in the middle of the squares below, and for each one of the questions identify some key words that will help you structure your ideas.

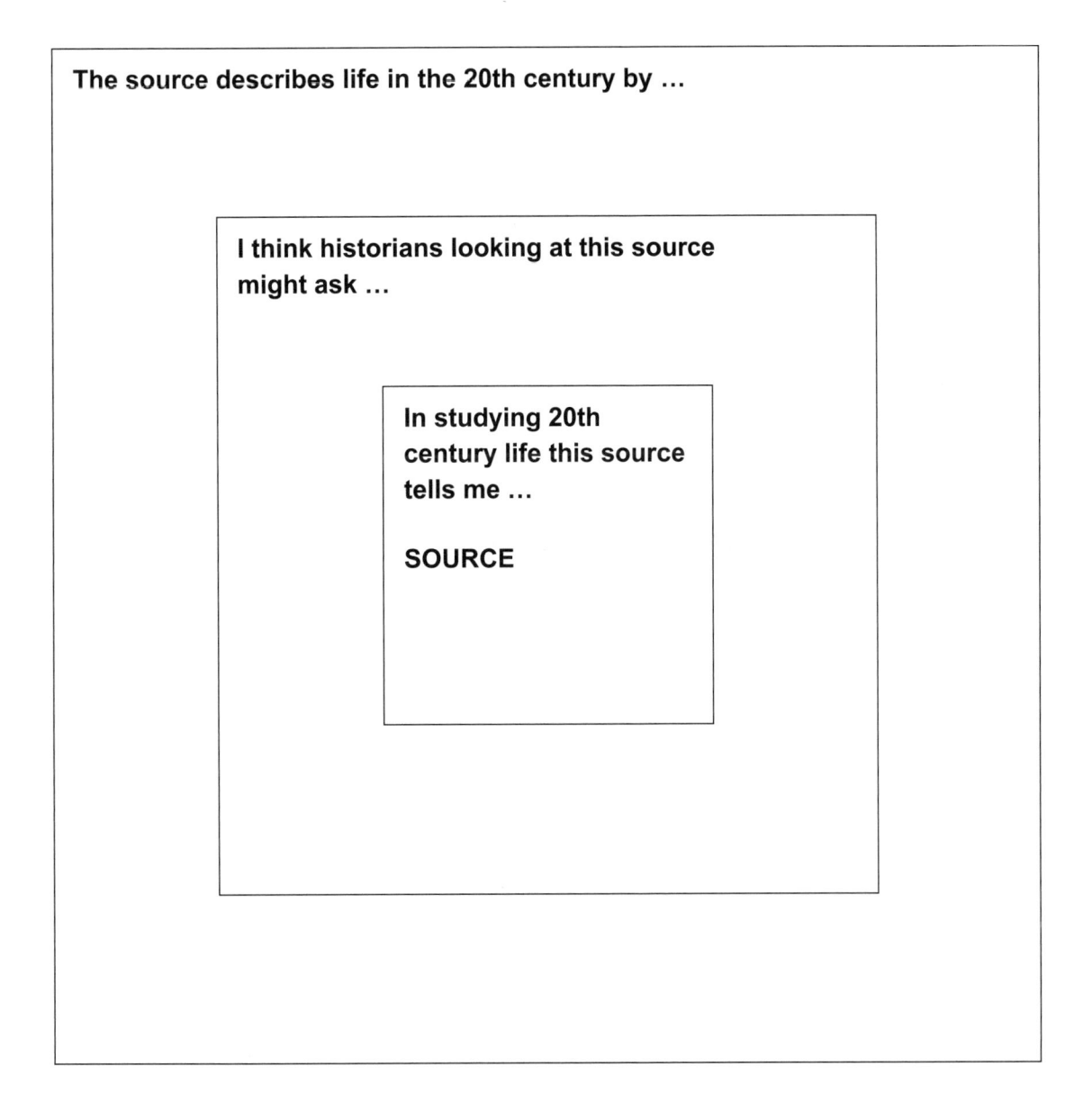

The source describes life in the 20th century by …

I think historians looking at this source might ask …

In studying 20th century life this source tells me …

SOURCE

Once you have finished your comments on this source pass it to another member of your group to add any other information.

If you think something that someone has added is incorrect, put a line through it and put your initials beside it. You will need to explain your change later.

> 2 Living and working

Unit 2 Assessment 2

Worksheet 2.13 (2) What was life like in the twentieth century?

How did you do?

Level 5: I was able to ...

suggest reasons for different interpretations of the past	
investigate historical problems and begin to ask my own questions	
evaluate sources to in order to establish evidence	
select and use information as well as use the correct historical words to support and structure my work.	

Level 6: I was able to ...

begin to explain how and why different interpretations of the past have been made	
investigate historical problems and begin to ask my own questions as part of the enquiry	
evaluate sources to establish evidence important to my enquiry	
select, organise, and use information, including the correct historical words, to produce structured work.	

Level 7: I was able to ...

explain how and why different interpretations of the past have been made	
investigate historical problems and issues by asking focused questions, and reflect on what I have done	
establish evidence for an enquiry by considering the origin, type and purpose of the sources	
select, organise and use the right information and the correct historical words to produce well-structured work.	

Things I did well: _____

I need to learn more about: _____

One thing I could do to improve is: _____

I will do this by: _____

Pupil comment: _____

_____

_____

Teacher comment: _____

_____

3 Moving and travelling

3.1 Who answered the call to war?

3.1a For King and Country, 1914–18?

Learning objectives
- To find out who travelled to support Britain in the First World War.
- To investigate a historical issue and set your own questions.

Historical background
Britain's declaration of war in August 1914, was followed by pledges of support from across the Empire. Men and women from all corners of the globe volunteered to serve the Mother Country; 329,000 Australians, 117,000 New Zealanders and 15,200 West Indians were amongst the approximate 1.5 million Empire troops who fought for Britain. Their motives for volunteering were varied, some volunteered out of a sense of duty, others sought adventure, and many welcomed the opportunity to travel.

Teaching Activities and Learning Outcomes

Assessment Opportunity and Homework

Investigating a historical issue.

Pupils will be able to

- ask questions about the topic
- refine those questions in the light of points made
- answer the refined questions.

Starter

Pupils look at **source a** (page 146, *History in Progress – Book 3*), and suggest what message is being conveyed. How is the message put across? At whom is it directed?

Development

Green task: After studying **sources b–e** (pages 146–147), pupils come up with three questions about support for Britain from the Empire. They are given advice on how to structure these questions.

Blue task: Pupils then share their questions with another pupil. They are given clear advice on how to revise questions.

Orange task: Pupils now try and answer their questions. They might be able to get enough information from the sources to answer their questions. However, they might wish to use the internet as a research tool to gain more detailed information.

Plenary

Pupils contribute to a whole class discussion about which questions worked well and how could they be best answered. An alternative plenary might be to ask pupils what they think were the most important reasons why people from across the globe volunteered to serve.

ICT opportunities

There are considerable opportunities for research about support for Britain from across the Empire using a number of websites. Go to www.heinemann.co.uk/hotlinks for a full list of websites.

> 3 Moving and travelling

3.1 Who answered the call to war?

3.1b What was the reaction in Britain to the arrival of Empire troops?

Learning objectives
- To find out about the reaction in Britain to help from abroad.
- To evaluate the use of newspapers as part of this enquiry.

Historical background
People from across the Empire were welcomed in Britain during the war because they had come to help. They served across the globe from France to Palestine, from India to the high seas. In late 1918, and during 1919, many Empire soldiers spent time in Britain before travelling home. This was a period of readjustment and, whilst the contribution from the Empire was highly praised in some quarters, the presence of people from across the world caused tension and occasionally outbursts of violence. The newspapers of the time reported both the praise and the problems

Teaching Activities and Learning Outcomes

Assessment opportunity

Evaluating newspapers as evidence

Pupils will be able to

- extract information from newspaper sources
- choose the most useful source
- evaluate newspapers as evidence.

Starter

What are newspapers useful for? Ask pupils to come up with three reasons why newspapers might be useful to historians.

Development

Green task: Ask pupils to read through **sources a–d** (pages 148–149). They should write down two or three points of what they consider to be useful information from each source.

Blue task: Pupils should attempt to evaluate the utility of the newspapers by asking a number of questions. To help the pupils, questions are included in the task box focussing on the information given, omission, scope and purpose of the evidence. The pupils can use **Worksheet 3.1b** for this exercise. They then need to choose their most useful extract and explain why they chose it.

Orange task: There is a word limit to this task to encourage the pupils to be concise in their responses. The pupils can write or type their responses to the question about the utility of newspapers.

Plenary

Class vote: Which was the most useful extract for the historian trying to find out about the reaction of the British public to the contribution of people from the Empire to the war effort?

Cross-curricular links

Citizenship: Race relations.

3.1 Who answered the call to war?

Worksheet 3.1b What was the reaction in Britain to the arrival of Empire troops?

1. Read each of the newspaper cuttings (**sources a–d**, pages 148–149 of *History in Progress – Book 3*). Write down two or three useful points of information from each source in the table below.
2. Complete the table by pointing out what points of information have been left out and whether the focus of the article is local or national. You should then comment on the purpose of the article, is it to inform, to criticise or to praise?

source	Information given	Possible information left out	Local or national?	Purpose	Summary: How useful?
a					
b					
c					
d					

© Pearson Education Ltd 2009: History in Progress – Planning and Resource Pack 3

3 Moving and travelling

3.2 How can moving make you safe?

3.2a What was Kindertransport?

Learning objectives
- To find out Kindertransport did to keep Jewish children safe.
- To use investigative skills to solve a problem.

Historical background

In November 1938, there were two nights of destruction and violence against Jews in Germany and Austria, now known as Kristallnacht (Night of the Broken Glass). The British government introduced a scheme known as Kindertransport (children's transport), whereby Jewish refugee children were given safe passage to Britain. They were sent to foster families, orphanages, group homes and farms. Up to 10,000 unaccompanied children and teenagers from Germany, Austria, Poland and Czechoslovakia arrived in the UK. Many had no time to say goodbye to their parents and most never saw them again.

The bronze sculpture (**source a**, page 150, *History in Progress – Book 3*) was designed by Frank Meisler, an Israeli artist who was himself a Kindertransport refugee. Round the base of the sculpture are the names of the towns from which the children came.

Teaching Activities and Learning Outcomes

Assessment opportunity

Inference drawing to solve a problem

Pupils will be able to

- use a sculpture to prompt considerations and work in pairs to develop questioning
- make inferences from sources to solve a problem
- use a particular style of writing to convey information.

Starter

Discuss whether pupils have been away without their parents. How did they feel? Explore the idea of being taken from home and family, sent to another country, not knowing where you will end up.

Development

Green task: Working in pairs, pupils draw up a list of questions they want to ask about the sculpture. Aim to have a class list of questions and discuss these as a transition to the blue task. Pupils should enter the most significant ones onto the question grid on **Worksheet 3.2a**, to be checked off later.

Blue task: Pupils work in pairs / small groups on **task 2** to sort out the information. **Worksheet 3.2a** may help here. Pupils then move on to **task 3**: identifying questions still to be answered using the sorting grid.

Orange task: Pupils are able to develop journalistic styles of writing. Encourage graphic skills.

Plenary

Reference back to the unanswered questions on the sorting grid, or ask pupils to read out different and contrastive journalistic write-ups of Kindertransport.

Cross-curricular links

Citizenship: The nature of our responsibility to others.

Religious studies: Persecution of the Jews.

English: Writing in a specific style.

ICT opportunities

ICT: designing and writing a newspaper article

3.2 How can moving make you safe?

Worksheet 3.2a What was Kindertransport?

1 Use the table below to list the questions you want to ask about the sculpture and keep track of whether you feel they have been answered.

Question	Has the question been answered?	What is the answer?

2 Use the sorting grid below to help you sort out the contents of the backpack. Once you have done so, make some notes in the space below about how these contents link to the House of Commons plaque.

Item	What does this tell me?
Photograph of wrecked synagogue	
Hitler Youth membership card	
Fabric yellow star of David	
Exit visa	
Photograph of Jewish children arriving in Harwich	
Letters tied in bundle	
Front cover of exercise book	
Pages from a diary	

How are the backpack's items linked to the House of Commons' plaque?

> 3 Moving and travelling

3.2 How can moving make you safe?

3.2b What motivated Oskar Schindler?

Learning objectives
- To find out what Oskar Schindler did to keep Jews safe.
- To reflect on Schindler's motives.

Historical Background

In 1908, Oskar Schindler was born into a wealthy industrialist family in Bohemia that suffered greatly in the Depression, causing Schindler to join the Nazi party. Following the German invasion of Poland, Schindler acquired a factory in Krakau. He had around 1,300 Jewish slave labourers producing enamelware. In 1942, he witnessed a Nazi raid on the Krakow ghetto and became active in saving his workers. Schindler was arrested twice for conspiracy but bribery enabled him to avoid jail. As the Red Army advanced, Nazis began to exterminate concentration camp inmates. In October 1944, Schindler managed to move 1,200 of his workers to Brunnlitz in Sudetenland. When a contingent of Jews was misrouted to Aushwitz, Schindler was able to have them returned to him. After the war he emigrated to Argentina, returning to Germany in 1958. He died in Hildersham, Germany, in 1974 and is buried in the catholic cemetery in Jerusalem. He is honoured in Israel's Yad Vashem memorial to the Holocaust.

Teaching Activities and Learning Outcomes.

Assessment opportunity

Empathetic understanding resulting in a consideration of motive.

Pupils will be able to

- ask inferences from a source and consider its universality
- empathise with an individual creating explanations for seemingly contradictory situations
- consider differing interpretations and weigh evidence to show support for one.

Starter

Discuss if one individual can make a difference. These differences can be for good or ill, and the individuals can be local, national or international.

Development

Green task: The whole task can be taken as an oral plenary, or pupils could work in pairs, sharing their ideas with the rest of the class on completion of the task.

Blue task: Pupils could work in pairs or small groups. One outcome could be two mini drama presentations to the class.

Orange task: This task gives pupils the opportunity to reflect upon motive and to back up their instincts by a consideration of the given source material. The first part of the task should be worked through individually with a written outcome.

Plenary

The final question 'Do motives matter as long as the result is good?' could be used as a whole class plenary, focusing as it does on the universal question of whether or not ends justify means.

Cross-curricular links

Citizenship: Do ends justify means?

Religious studies: Persecution of the Jews

English: Drama

3 Moving and travelling

3.2 How can moving make you safe?

3.2c Adam Rybczynski's story

Learning objectives
- To find out how the Second World War affected Adam Rybcynski.
- To identify and explain the gaps in Adam's story.

Historical background

Adam Rybczynski was born in 1909, in the Wolyn region of Eastern Europe within the Russian empire. By 1920, boundaries had been redrawn; Adam's village was in the newly independent Poland. After the Soviet invasion of Poland on 17 September 1939, the village became part of the Soviet Union. Adam and his family, along with over 1 million Poles, were now considered enemies of the Soviet Union and were sent to labour camps. In June 1941, Germany attacked the Soviet Union and Stalin made an alliance with Britain. No longer seen as enemies, the Poles were released from the camps. Adam joined the new Polish army being formed under General Anders. It was made up of Poles who had been prisoners of the Nazis and wanted to fight for their country. In 1942, he left Soviet territory to train alongside the British army. When the war ended, Adam, like thousands of other Poles, chose exile in Britain, separating himself from his family. He died in 1980. It's unknown if he ever returned to visit his village.

Teaching Activities and Learning Outcomes

Assessment opportunity

Chronological understanding.

Pupils will be able to

- create a chronology from a source
- use a chronology to identify gaps and ask questions with the aim of filling those gaps
- work with sources to develop and enhance a chronology.

Starter

Quick-fire round: why were people on the move after the war? Expect / encourage 'troops returning home', 'Jews were looking for a secure home', 'Germans leaving occupied territories' and 'people fleeing from newly established communist regimes in Eastern Europe'. Focus on the personal impact.

Development

Green task: Using **source a** (page 154 of *History in Progress – Book 3*), pupils work in pairs to draw up a chronology of Adam's life. They could compare their list with others to build up a complete chronology as possible. The Alien Registration Certificate is reproduced on **Worksheet 3.2c (1)**.

Blue task: For **task 2**, pupils work individually or in pairs to create a detailed chronology using the Fact Cards on **Worksheet 3.2c (2)**. Creating a chronology could involve sorting cards onto a timeline, either as hard copy or using IT. **Task 3a** and **b** could be a plenary once the chronologies have been completed.

Orange task: In **task 4**, pupils reflect upon Adam's life and how two sources can be used to suggest the continuation of family relationships. The Red Cross Letter is reproduced on **Worksheet 3.2c (3)**.

Plenary

Use **task 5** of the orange task as a plenary. Encourage discussion, but be aware of pupil sensibilities.

Cross-curricular links

Citizenship: What it means to belong to a place and whether this is important.

ICT opportunities

Creating a timeline.

3 Moving and travelling

3.2 How can moving make you safe?

Worksheet 3.2c (1) Adam Rybczynski's story

Nationality: Polish
Born on 10.11.09 in Kudryn Buderaz
Previous Nationality (if any): Russian
Profession or Occupation: Labourer
Single or Married: Married
Address of Residence: 13, Fairlight Avenue, Ramsgate.
Arrival in United Kingdom on: —
Address of last Residence outside U.K.: Polish Forces in Italy.
Government Service: Served in Polish Army from Sept., 1942 until 3.3.47.
Passport or other papers as to Nationality and Identity: Army Form X204 (Polish)

Registration Certificate No. A.576023
Issued at: Ramsgate, Kent
on 25th May, 1954.
Name (Surname first in Roman Capitals): RYBCZYNSKI, Adam
Alias:
Left Thumb Print (if unable to sign name in English Characters).
Signature of Holder: Adam Rybczynski

3.2 How can moving make you safe?

Worksheet 3.2c (2) Adam Rybczynski's story

2 Cut out the fact cards below to help sort and order the chronology of Adam's life.

| Adam was born in 1909 in a village of the Wolyn region of Eastern Europe in what was then the Russian Empire. | By 1920 the Wolyn region was part of independent Poland. | In September 1939 the Russian army invaded Poland and Adam's village became part of the Soviet Union. |

| Adam, his wife and all his family, along with 1 million other Poles, were sent to labour camps deep inside the Soviet Union. Thousands died from exhaustion and starvation. | In June 1941 Nazi Germany attacked Soviet Russia. Britain and the Soviet Union became allies. The Russians could no longer treat the Poles as enemies. | In September 1941 Adam joined a new Polish army led by General Anders. It was made up of Poles who had been prisoners of the Russians and who wanted to fight for their country. |

| In 1942 Adam left the Soviet Union to train alongside the British army. He served as a driver in the 'Anders Army' and fought at the Battle of Monte Cassino in 1944. | At the end of the Second World War, national boundaries in Europe were re-drawn. Adam's village was now in communist Ukraine. Adam was afraid to go home. | Along with thousands of other Poles, Adam decided to stay in Britain. He died in 1980. |

3 Moving and travelling

3.2 How can moving make you safe?

Worksheet 3.2c (3) Adam Rybczynski's story

THE BRITISH RED CROSS SOCIETY
14 & 15, GROSVENOR CRESCENT,
LONDON, S.W.1.

Telephone:
SLOANE 5191

Cables:
BRITREDCROSS, LONDON

Telegrams:
REDCROS, KNIGHTS, LONDON

Patron & President: HER MAJESTY THE QUEEN
Vice-President: HER MAJESTY QUEEN ELIZABETH THE QUEEN MOTHER.

Executive Committee
Chairman: THE RIGHT HON. VISCOUNT WOOLTON, P.C., C.H., D.L.
Vice-Chairman: THE COUNTESS OF LIMERICK, D.B.E., LL.D.
Deputy Chairman: MRS. A. M. BRYANS, C.B.E.
Secretary General: F. H. D. PRITCHARD, ESQ.

MEW/VG/Polish   29th November, 1954.

Mr. Adam Rybczynski.

        Mr. Jozef RYBCZYNSKI

Dear Sir,

    We have received an enquiry from the Comite International de la Croix-Rouge in Geneva on behalf of your father, Mr. Jozef Rybczynski, Plawna Gorna, pta Plawna, pow. Lwowek Slaski, woj. Wroclaw, Poland, who is anxious to hear from you.

    We should be grateful if you would let us know whether you will be writing to your father and whether we may give the Comite International de la Croix-Rouge your address for onward transmission to him.

    We shall be glad if you will acknowledge this letter so that we may know it has reached you safely. We would not send your address to Mr. Rybczynski without first having received your permission to do so.

                      Yours faithfully,

                    (Mrs.) M. E. Wetherall
                 International Welfare Section
          International Relations and Relief Department.

3.2 How can moving make you safe?

3.2d What was Exodus 1947?

Learning objectives
- To find out about the journey made by *Exodus 1947* in July 1947.
- To conduct an investigation into the purpose of the voyage of the *Exodus 1947*.

Historical background
The League of Nations, charged with securing a Jewish national home, whilst protecting the civil and religious rights of Arabs and Jews, placed Palestine under British administration. In 1919, the population of Palestine was almost entirely Arab. Jewish persecution in Germany led to an increase in legal and illegal immigrants. The *Exodus 47* was acquired by the Mosad le-Aliya Bet with the intention of mounting an illegal operation, grabbing the attention of the world's press and influencing the United Nations Special Committee on Palestine. Carrying 4,500 Jewish refugees from Europe to Palestine in the final year of the British Mandate, the ship became a symbol for unrestricted Jewish immigration to Palestine, and highlighted the need for a Jewish homeland. The committee recommended partition. On 14 May 1948, the state of Israel was proclaimed. Hostilities between Israel and Palestine have existed ever since.

Teaching Activities and Learning Outcomes

Assessment opportunity

Source evaluation to determine motive.

Pupils will be able to

- contextualise a specific source, using given information
- evaluate source material
- use a particular style of writing to convey information.

Starter

Quick-fire round: what does 'exodus' mean? Recap on the fact that once the Second World War was over there were vast movements of people. Focus on Jews seeking a safe homeland as a transition.

Development

Green task: Focus on **source a** (page 156, *History in Progress – Book 3*). Pupils work individually or in pairs to draw up responses to **tasks 1** and **2** and then share conclusions (**Worksheet 3.2d**).

Blue task: Pupils work in pairs or individually on **tasks 3** and **4**, or, if time is pressing, they could be undertaken in a plenary session. The table on **Worksheet 3.2d** will help. Pupils may need reminding about the Nazi connections implied by the swastika on the flag. **Task 5** should be done individually.

Orange task: Pupils are able to develop journalistic styles of writing. Encourage graphic skills.

Plenary

The 'Back to the Start' discussion could be used as the final plenary

Cross-curricular links

Citizenship: The nature of our responsibility to others; what nationhood means: can a nation thrive without a homeland?

Religious studies: Persecution of the Jews

English: Writing in a specific style; propaganda

ICT opportunities

Designing and writing a newspaper article.

3 Moving and travelling

3.2 How can moving make you safe?

Worksheet 3.2d What was Exodus 1947?

1a–c Use the table below to help sort out your conclusions of the ship from **source a** (page 156, *History in Progress – Book 3*).

Condition of the ship	Conclusions	Clues about purpose of voyage

2 Are there any further questions you would like to ask as part of your investigation?

1 _____

2 _____

3 _____

Was it all a propaganda stunt?

3a Use the table below to help you compare **sources b** and **c** (pages 156–157, *History in Progress – Book 3*).

	source b (statement from crew)	source c (interview with captain)
Type of battle		
Length of battle		
Casualties		
Role of Mossad		

3b Use the table below to help you compare the reliability of the two sources.

Reliability questions	source b (crew's statement)	source c (captain's interview)
There at the time?		
Took part in action?		
One person's view?		
View of many?		
Reporting at the time?		
Reporting later?		
Knowledge of motives behind the sailing?		

3.3 How did the British rule in India come to an end?

3.3a Why did the British leave India in 1947?

Learning objectives
- To consider the significance of Gandhi to the end of the British rule in India.
- To make a judgement using a range of information.

Historical background
At the height of the British Raj, before the First World War, only 1,500 British civil servants ruled an Indian population of 400 million, but it seemed inconceivable that India would gain its independence in the twentieth century. Then, due to a combination of changes (in the trade and financial relations between Britain and India, in the geopolitical view of imperialism, and above all the impact of two world wars), the British began to concede more and more political powers. Still, many Indians were frustrated and began to launch radical campaigns to achieve complete independence. Gandhi spent a total of 2,338 days in prison because of his opposition to British rule. These campaigns failed to drive the British out of India, but they did put a strain on their ability to rule and contributed to a departure far earlier than most expected.

Teaching Activities and Learning Outcomes

Homework

There is much more to learn about the Indian struggle for freedom. Ask pupils to find out more about Ghandi and other important figures (such as Jawaharlal Nehru, Subhas Chandra Bose, Muhammad Ali Jinnah, Viceroy Mountbatten, Annie Besant) and create a poster or mini-book about them.

Assessment opportunity

Considering the significance of important individuals in their historical context; analysing and explaining the reasons for, and results of, historical events, situations and changes.

Pupils will be able to

- explain how Gandhi hoped to achieve Indian independence and if his ideas and methods worked
- create an argument concerning the significance of Gandhi in the Indian attainment of independence.

Starter

Pupils look at **sources a** and **b** (page 158 of *History in Progress – Book 3*), and note the ways in which Gandhi's appearance changed. Discuss what clothes say about a person, and what Gandhi is saying about himself in each photo. Ask pupils to think of reasons why his appearance changed so radically.

Development

Green task: Pupils complete this task individually or in pairs (**Worksheet 3.3a**).

Blue task: Pupils should use the methods they identified in **task 1** to fill in the column headers (the methods should be along the lines of 'unity of all Indians', 'boycott British things', 'non-violent protest'). **Worksheet 3.3a** will help structure their work. Explain that not necessarily every event will allow us to judge Gandhi's methods, should this be the case they should leave the box blank.

Orange task: Pupils could complete this task on paper or using ICT facilities if available. Make it clear that pupils are constructing an interpretation of Gandhi's importance; they do not have to sit on the fence with their language or their argument.

Plenary

Look again at **sources a** and **b** on page 158. Have you changed your reasons for why he might have changed his appearance?

ICT opportunities

Task 3 could be completed using ICT facilities; homework might include internet research.

3 Moving and travelling

3.3 How did the British rule in India come to an end?

Worksheet 3.3a Why did the British leave India in 1947?

1 Read through the following extract from Gandhi's book *Hind Swaraj*. Underline or draw arrows to highlight the different methods Gandhi planned to use to free India from British rule.

> The British have not taken India: we have given it to them! We strengthen their hold by arguing amongst ourselves. We were one nation before the British came to India; they have divided Hindus and Muslims, but we must stand together once more. We must say to the British 'you can only rule us as long as we wished to be ruled; soon we shall no longer have any dealings with you'. We must boycott British tax, schools, law courts, and trade. We must spin our own cloth and refuse to buy British machine-made clothes. But we must not use violence. Violence only leads to more misery and is not natural to the Indian soil. We must defeat the British with passive resistance; we must win our freedom by showing the world that we are brave enough to suffer British anger.

2 Read through the seven steps to independence on page 159 of *History in Progress – Book 3*. Use the information, together with the methods you identified in **task 1**, to complete the table below. Remember to give each method a mark out of 5 (1 showing that the method worked well, 5 showing the method failed). Explain the mark you have given.

Event	Method:	Method:	Method:
The Montagu Speech			
Massacre at Amritsar			
Non-cooperation			
The Salt March			
The Round Table Conference			
Second World War			
Independence Day			

3.3 How did the British rule in India come to an end?

3.3b Why did 12 million Indians leave their homes in 1947?

Learning objectives
- To explore reasons for the refugee crisis of 1947–48.
- To extract information from different types of source to explain a problem.

Historical background
Indian politicians and historians have accused the British of pursuing a deliberate policy of divide and rule throughout the devolution of power; separate electorates were created for Hindu, Muslims and Sikhs at local, provincial and then imperial levels of government. Censuses further re-enforced ideas of communal separation. Lord Louis Mountbatten, the last viceroy of India, came up with a number of plans (including the 'balkanisation' of India) that were rejected, before all sides (except Gandhi) accepted the idea of partition. As soon as the partition plan was announced on 3 June 1947, violence began to occur. Sir Cyril Radcliffe was pressured to rush his task of establishing the new international boundaries and expressed distress about the consequences of his work as he finished on 13 August. Leaders were powerless to control the violence which erupted on the stroke of midnight on 15 August. By 1948, 12 million people had become refugees, with an estimated death toll of 1 million.

Teaching Activities and Learning Outcomes

Assessment opportunity
Analysing and explaining reasons for historical events; evaluating the comparative use of different sources to investigate and explain historical events.

Pupils will be able to
- extract information from a range of sources to explain the refugee crisis of 1947–48
- compare and contrast information in a range of sources
- evaluate which type of source is of most use in understanding the refugee crisis of 1947–48.

Starter
Pupils look at **source a** on page 160 of *History in Progress – Book 3*. Ask them to pick out details of what they can see going on in the cartoon. Then ask for suggestions on why the cartoonist included these details. After this, ask the pupils what they think the overall message of the cartoon is.

Development
Green task: Pupils can complete this task individually or in pairs. Encourage pupils to extract specific information from each of the sources. **Worksheet 3.3b** will help structure research.

Blue task: Ask pupils to compare and contrast the information they used to complete the previous task. Again, pupils could use **Worksheet 3.3b** to structure their answer.

Orange task: Encourage pupils to consider the content and the provenance of the source when considering how useful it is for the proposed research. Instruct pupils to follow the clear guidance of the orange box when completing this task.

Plenary
Ask the class to look back over this enquiry and enquiry **3.3a**, discuss how far they think the British are to blame for the violent way in which the Raj came to an end in 1947?

Cross-curricular links
Religious studies: On what theological and cultural grounds do Hinduism and Islam differ?

3 Moving and travelling

3.3 How did the British rule in India come to an end?

Worksheet 3.3b Why did 12 million Indians leave their homes in 1947?

1 Look at the map and **sources a–d** (pages 161–162, *History in Progress – Book 3*). Use information or details from each source to fill in the first column in the table below:

Source	Details that help to explain the outbreak of violence:	Examples of where details from other sources support this source
a		
b		
c		
e		
Map		

2 Now look at the information you have taken from the sources. To complete the table, find as many points as you can where the information from one source supports that in another source (this is called cross-referencing).

3 I would send source____. This is because _____

_____

_____

_____

_____

_____

3 Moving and travelling

3.4 Why did people leave their homelands?

3.4a What effect did the arrival of the SS *Empire Windrush* have?

Learning objectives
- To find out about the experiences of black people from the West Indies who came to live and work in Britain at the end of the 1940s.
- To weigh up the problems facing immigrants.

Historical background
After the Second World War the British government wanted to start rebuilding so they decided to recruit labour from the Caribbean to help overcome the shortage in British industries. In 1948, an advertisement was placed in a Jamaican newspaper and when the *Empire Windrush* arrived in Jamaica, all 300 places had been taken. An extra 192 places were created for those who were prepared to spend the voyage on deck. Many were ex-servicemen who wished to re-join. Others looked for a better life and work opportunities as unemployment in Jamaica was high. When the *Windrush* passengers arrived in Britain, they were faced with the problem of accommodation. A disused air-raid shelter in Clapham Common became a temporary solution for 230 of the arrivals. The nearest employment exchange was Brixton, and as a result many settled there, making it one of Britain's first Caribbean communities. There was plenty of work available in Britain and, although black Caribbean workers were kept out of the higher-paid jobs, many were absorbed into public sector jobs: in hospitals, the Post Office, London Transport and the railways. By 1955, 18,000 Jamaicans had moved to Britain.

Teaching Activities and Learning Outcomes

Assessment opportunity

Analysing sources to determine outcomes and suggest rectification

Pupils will be able to

- extract information from sources and use it to determine motive
- link the consequences of an event
- weigh and rank advantages and disadvantages of specific courses of action.

Starter

Ask pupils to look at **source a** (page 162, *History in Progress – Book 3*) and to consider what the new arrivals are thinking and feeling. Remind pupils the immigrants' thoughts and emotions would depend very much on why they had made the journey. Use this as a transition to the green task.

Development

Green task: Working individually, or in pairs, pupils draw up a list of reasons why the Jamaicans came to Britain [**Worksheet 3.4a (1)**]. Individual / group lists can then be compared and a class list compiled.

Blue task: Pupils start by focusing on **sources f–i** (page 164, *History in Progress – Book 3*) and extract consequences from them which are then linked on a spider diagram [**Worksheet 3.4a (1)**]. Pupils could work in pairs on **tasks 2** and **3**, but should complete **task 4** individually.

Orange task: Pupils work in pairs to rank the 'solutions' to ending racism and prejudice. Their reasons for the ranking can be given orally or noted down [**Worksheet 3.4a (2)**].

Plenary

Moving on from the orange task, pupils reflect on ways in which racism and prejudice can be ended.

Cross-curricular links

Citizenship: The nature of racism and prejudice and how it can be ended.

3 Moving and travelling

3.4 Why did people leave their homelands?

Worksheet 3.4a (1) What effect did the arrival of the SS *Empire Windrush* have?

1a Using **sources b–e** on page 163 of *History in Progress – Book 3*, make a list of why people decided to travel to Britain on the Empire Windrush. Once you have your list, decide if they were push, or pull factors.

	Reasons for travelling to Britain	Push or pull factor?
source b		
source c		
source d		
source e		

2 Look at **sources b–i** on pages 163–164 of *History in Progress – Book 3*. Use the table below to help sort your ideas about the consequences of immigration

Consequence	source f	source g	source h	source i
Consequence 1				
Consequence 2				
Consequence 3				

Link the consequences on a spider diagram.

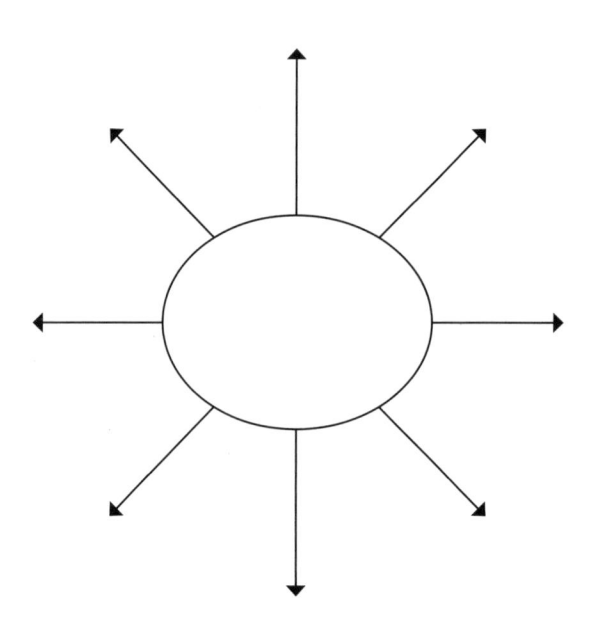

3.4 Why did people leave their homelands?

Worksheet 3.4a (2) What effect did the arrival of the SS *Empire Windrush* have?

1 Legislation

1965: Racial discrimination in public places prohibited.

1968: Racial discrimination in areas such as housing and employment illegal.

1976: Illegal to encourage racial hatred.

2010: ???

2 Community Projects

Working together as a community to, for example, decorate an old people's day centre, tidy up a graveyard or organise a carnival.

3 Sport

Support mixed-race national teams.

4 Entertainment

Listen to and enjoy West Indian performers.

5 Education

Teach about the history of black people and make sure that every school has a proportion of black children in it.

> 3 Moving and travelling

3.4 Why did people leave their homelands?

3.4b British and Asian: a clash of cultures?

Learning objectives
- To weigh up how far South Asian culture has clashed with British culture since the 1960s.
- To research and prepare a script using a range of sources.

Historical background
South Asian migration to Britain began in the seventeenth century as the East India Company hired lascars (Indian sailors or militiamen) who sometimes settled in London. By the turn of the twentieth century there were around 70,000 Indians living in Britain. Many manual workers came over from Pakistan after the Second World War; industrial work also tempted many Punjabis to settle in northern England in the 1950s and 1960s. These groups were joined by Indians expelled from East Africa in the 1960s and 1970s. The Commonwealth Immigrants Act of 1962 and the Immigration Act of 1971 restricted immigration to those who already had family in Britain. The 2001 Census recorded just over 2 million South Asians living in the UK, around 4% of the population. The birth of second and third generation British Asians has accounted for most of the population increase.

Teaching Activities and Learning Outcomes

Assessment opportunity

Understanding the diverse experiences, ideas, beliefs, and attitudes of people from different cultures; communicating knowledge of history in various ways using correct chronology and historical vocabulary.

Pupils will be able to

- use a range of different sources to weigh up whether there has been a clash or a fusion of British and Asian cultures
- write a script for a radio documentary about the experience of Asians in Britain since the 1960s.

Starter

Pupils look at **source a** (page 166 of *History in Progress – Book 3*). In pairs, and then as a class, ask pupils to list the ways in which the photo appears to show a clash or a fusion of cultures. You could ask pupils to think of local examples of a clash or fusion of cultures (not necessarily South Asian) and more generally to consider how far it is possible to have a 'multi-cultural' society.

Development

Green task: Pupils could do this task individually or discuss the sources in pairs (**Worksheet 3.4b**).

Blue task: Pupils could discuss this in pairs before answering this task. Ask pupils to think about which source offers the best evidence for their answer (**Worksheet 3.4b**)

Orange task: Encourage pupils to produce a chatty script, complete with a typical introduction. The pupils could be encouraged to use guests as a means of working some of the evidence from the sources into their programme. The pupils could actually record their programme if resources are available.

Plenary

Snowball the question comparing South Asian and West Indian immigration. Pupils agree about whether there are more similarities or differences in pairs, fours, eights and finally as a class.

Cross-curricular links

Citizenship: Exploring what it means to be British, is it possible to have a 'multi-cultural' society?

PSHE: Exploring attitudes to race and racism in Britain.

3.4 Why did people leave their homelands?

Worksheet 3.4b British and Asian: a clash of cultures?

1 Look at **sources b–g** on pages 166–167 of *History in Progress – Book 3*. Use the information in the sources to complete the table below.

Source	Fusion or Clash?	Details from the source that support this:
b		
c		
d		
e		
f		
g		

2 Use the research in your table to complete the answer below:

Overall, the sources better support the conclusion that there has been a _____ of British and Asian culture. The best example of this is _____

_____

_____

_____

_____

3 Moving and travelling

3.4 Why did people leave their homelands?

3.4c Taking it further!: Why were British children sent to Australia?

Learning objectives
- Use the given sources as evidence for reactions to child migrants to Australia.

Historical background
Between 1950 and 1967, under a policy of child migration, thousands of children were sent, with government approval, by church organisations and charities to Commonwealth countries such as Australia, New Zealand and Canada. About 150,000 children were taken to Australia. The children were classed as orphans despite the fact that most were not. They came mainly from poor families or had been born to unmarried mothers. Frequently, the children were only supposed to be in care for a short period because their nuclear families couldn't cope. Often the families hadn't even agreed to migration but to adoption instead, which didn't happen. The children were usually told that their parents were dead, and were given new names when they arrived at their destination. Once abroad, the children were often used as cheap labour or became the victims of physical or sexual abuse. Traumatised, the children, when adults, sought restitution and reunion with their families.

Assessment Opportunity
Working with source material, making inferences and backing their views with evidence.

Starter
Look at the photograph of children arriving in Australia (**source a**, page 168 of *History in Progress – Book 3*). Quick-fire round the group: one word to describe the photograph.

Development
Task 1: requires comprehension and inference-making from the first two sources, along with cross-referencing.

Task 2: invite speculation, but aim to keep pupils' ideas within the bounds of possibility

Task 3: requires cross-referencing to lesson 3.4a and a consideration of motive. In dealing with all tasks, the quality of support for the view given is what is important.

Plenary
Take **task 4** as a plenary and ask pupils to consider whether apologies should only be made to the living, or by people directly involved. Looking further back in time, ask whether the British should apologise for the slave trade, or the French for invading in 1066 etc.

Cross-curricular links
PSHE: Is it important to know who your family are?

3 Moving and travelling

3.5 How did African colonies gain independence?

3.5a Does Kwame Nkrumah deserve to be remembered as the 'Osagyefo' of Ghana?

Learning objectives
- To find out about the life and career of Kwame Nkrumah.
- To consider how far Nkrumah deserves to be remembered positively by Ghanaians.

Historical background
Ghana was the first sub-Saharan African country to gain its independence in 1957. The name Ghana was chosen to evoke memories of the great independent Kingdom of Ghana (790–1240 AD). The allusion to the old kingdom appealed to Nkrumah who saw himself as a modern black Caesar. The Portuguese were the first Europeans lured to 'the Gold Coast' and encountered the powerful Ashanti rulers in the fifteenth century. Britain fought a series of wars, primarily against the Dutch, between 1821 and 1901 to gain control over the gold supply. Due to the climate and disease, there were few British settlers, so the local population gained a comparatively excellent education to serve as administrators.

Teaching Activities and Learning Outcomes

Assessment opportunity

Considering the significance of important individuals in their historical context and in the present day; understanding why historians and others have interpreted people in different ways; organising and writing an argument that uses the correct chronology and historical vocabulary.

Pupils will be able to

- pick out relevant bits of information to support different interpretations of Nkrumah's significance
- consider why different interpretations of Nkrumah's reputation exist
- write a speech to argue for a particular interpretation of Nkrumah's reputation.

Starter

Ask pupils to look at **source a** (page 170 of *History in Progress – Book 3*) and think of three words to describe Nkrumah. Write suggestions on the board, perhaps grouping them into positive and negative descriptions. These words could be of use when the pupils come to answer **task 4**.

Development

Green task: Model the first boxes of the timeline (page 170) as a class, emphasise that not all the information will support either statement. Then pupils can work individually or in pairs (**Worksheet 3.5a**).

Blue task: Pupils can discuss **task 2a** in pairs, and then as a class. Explain that there are lots of different images of Nkrumah, but the website designers specifically chose this one: are they fans? Relatives? Do they have an agenda? Are there rival websites? What views and images of Nkrumah do they have? A vote, followed by a class discussion of **task 2b**, could generate ideas to help with **task 4**.

Orange task: Ask pupils if they have ever seen someone give a speech; what made it effective / not effective? Encourage pupils to use rhetorical tricks to make their speech powerful and persuasive: the use of three main arguments, repetition of phrases in threes, and perhaps some bombastic vocabulary!

Plenary

Ask for some volunteers to read their speeches (or just some exciting extracts from their speeches) to the class, some in favour or Nkrumah and some against.

ICT opportunities

Pupils could use the internet to research other representations of Nkrumah.

3 Moving and travelling

3.5 How did African colonies gain their independence?

Worksheet 3.5a Does Kwame Nkrumah deserve to be remembered as the 'Osagyefo' of Ghana?

1 Look at the timelines on pages 170–171 of *History in Progress – Book 3*. Use the information in the timelines to complete the table below.

Year	'Kwame Nkumah was very important in Ghana winning independence in 1957.'	'There were other reasons that explain Ghana's independence- not Nkrumah!'
1945	Nkrumah organised protests in England against the British Empire.	
By 1947		Indian independence was an important example to Ghanaians.

150 © Pearson Education Ltd 2009: History in Progress – Planning and Resource Pack 3

3 Moving and travelling

3.5 How did African colonies gain their independence?

3.5b Why did the Algerians fight for their freedom?

Learning objectives
- To explain why the Algerian struggle for independence led to war.
- To devise categories to organise lots of information.

Historical background

In 1830 the French invaded the Algiers; by 1834 they had occupied and annexed the whole of Algeria. After the First World War (in the wake of Algerian sacrifices for the French and encouraged by the idea of national self-determination as part of Wilson's 14 Points), many Algerians wanted greater autonomy. Any reform was opposed by the pieds-noirs. Tension increased after the Second World War; a VE Day celebration turned into a clash between Muslims and Europeans. Over 100 Europeans were killed and reprisal attacks that followed (the Sétif Massacre) left around 6000 Muslims dead. Relations deteriorated and the Federation Liberation Nationale (FLN) was formed in 1954. Six years later, after 700,000 deaths and the collapse of the Fourth Republic in 1958, Charles De Gaulle signed the Evian Accords granting Algeria independence. Ahmed Ben Bella, former leader of the FLN, became the first President of Algeria.

Teaching Activities and Learning Outcomes

Assessment opportunity

Making and testing hypotheses to investigate specific historical questions; analysing and explaining the reasons for historical events.

Pupils will be able to

- make links between pieces of information to help analyse a historical problem
- evaluate which causes of violence in Algeria were the most important.

Starter

Ask pupils to look at **source a** (page 172, *History in Progress – Book 3*) and describe what is happening and why. Suggestions might include 'the Algerians were angry' or 'the French wanted to crush opposition'. Make sure pupils expand on these ideas. Write ideas on the board to help with **task 1b**.

Development

Green task: Worksheet 3.5b or the *History in Progress – LiveText CD 3* can be used for this task.

Blue task: Discuss the criteria to be used before allowing the pupils to complete this task: what was the trigger? What was the point at which violence became inevitable? Encourage pupils to think of some boxes being of equal importance. Cut out cards should be marked to indicate which group they belong in before being ordered physically (using rows / pyramids to show those of equal importance).

Orange task: Pupils can use the categories from **task 1** to organise their paragraphs. They should use the comparative importance they discussed in **task 2** to structure the running order of those paragraphs, starting with the least important reason and building to the most important.

Plenary

Back to the start!: Look back at **Lesson 3.5a** and compare the violence in Algeria with the peace in Ghana. Discuss the reasons why the Ghanaians gained independence peacefully.

Cross-curricular links

Citizenship: Does violence ever help to achieve beneficial changes in society?

ICT opportunities

History in Progress – LiveText CD 3. www.heinemann.co.uk/hotlinks lists useful websites.

3 Moving and travelling

3.5 How did African colonies gain their independence?

Worksheet 3.5b Why did the Algerians fight for their freedom?

1a Draw lines between the boxes below that contain similar bits of information.

1b Label your lines with a category that explains the link between the boxes. One has been done for you as an example. (There are hints on page 172 of *History in Progress – Book 3* to help you with this task).

By 1954, France had ruled Algeria for 124 years

By 1954, there were 1 million pieds-noirs living in Algeria. They were totally against making deals with the native Algerians.

One-third of the people who lived in Algiers were French.

In 1954, the French Army lost a war to keep hold of the French colony Indo-China. They were angry, embarrassed and determined not to lose another colony.

Only eight out of 864 top government jobs were held by native Algerians

---

Eight MPs represented 1 million Algerian French in the French parliament. Another eight MPs represented 8 million native Algerians

---

Ahmed Ben Bella was an Algerian who fought for the French in the Second World War. He thought the French did not reward Algeria enough after the war. He led the FLN.

The native Algerian population doubled between 1900 and 1950. Many lived in shanty towns called 'bidonvilles'.

Algerians were angry

The Federation Liberation Nationale (FLN) were a group of Algerian terrorists who launched their first attack on 1 November 1954. They shot French military leaders.

The French Army began to kill native civilians and arrest whole villages to try and stop the FLN in November 1954.

The pieds-noirs said that the French government was not doing enough to help them. They formed their own armed gangs to fight native Algerians.

The FLN began to kill French civilians with guns and bombs in August 1955.

In 1956 the French increased the number of soldiers in Algeria from 100,000 to 500,000.

In 1956 the French discovered oil in the south of Algeria

In 1959 the French government tried to make a deal with the FLN - to allow a public vote on freedom if the violence stopped. The FLN and the pieds-noirs rejected this.

In 1961 some members of the French Army and the pieds-noirs formed the 'Secret Army' to attack native Algerian civilians.

3 Moving and travelling

3.5 How did African colonies gain their independence?

3.5c Taking it further!: Who is to blame for the problems in Zimbabwe?

Learning objectives
- To analyse the extent to which 'the West' is responsible for the current problems in Zimbabwe.

Historical background
This is covered in the enquiry itself. If you wish to learn more about Mugabe, read *R. Mugabe* by M. Meredith. There is an excellent section on Zimbabwe in Meredith's *The State of Africa*.

Teaching Activities and Learning Outcomes

Assessment opportunity

Analysing and explaining the reasons for historical events and changes in Zimbabwe.

Pupils will be able to

- plan and write an analytical essay about the causes of the current problems in Zimbabwe.

Starter

Ask the pupils which of the images on pages 174 and 175 of *History in Progress – Book 3*, is of more use in understanding what is wrong in modern Zimbabwe. There should be good arguments for and against both sources.

Development

Over to you...! Ask pupils what factors that could have caused the current problems in Zimbabwe have been mentioned in the text. Write these suggestions (such as British colonial legacy, Ian Smith, Mugabe, tribal differences) on the board. Ask the pupils to re-read the text and to pick out information that supports each of these factors. The pupils could construct a spider diagram to help with this phase. Then, ask the pupils to put the factors in order of their importance in causing the current problems; make sure you ask the pupils to justify their order in a whole class discussion. The pupils should then be ready to start their essays. Explain that the introduction should state their overall answer and outline the major factors to be considered. The pupils should then dedicate one paragraph to each factor, starting with the least important and building to the most important. Explain that the best answers will explain how some factors did contribute to the current problems, but also clearly explain why they cannot be thought of as the most important factor. The conclusion should clearly state why their most important factor has been primarily responsible for the current problems.

Plenary

Hot-seating: Select pupils to sit in a chair at the front of the class to face questions about Mugabe and Zimbabwe from their peers.

ICT opportunities

Pupils could use the internet to conduct further research into the history of Zimbabwe, Robert Mugabe and Zanu-PF, before answering the essay question.

3 Moving and travelling

3.6a Where can migration lead?

3.6a Why move from Africa to Hawaii?

Learning objectives
- To discover why people moved from Africa to the USA in the 1960s.
- To discover that an event can be interpreted in different ways.

Historical background
There was greater migration and mobility between continents after the Second World War, particularly between African and America. Aside from improvements in transport that reduced the time it took people to travel from one place to another, there were many other factors which encouraged greater migration. An increasingly global media raised opportunities of education and work elsewhere; emerging African nationalism emphasised the importance of education as a means of self improvement; institutions in the USA and Europe made scholarship and bursary funds available to African students; as the civil rights movement grew, racial barriers began to come down in America. Barack Obama's father belonged to the first generation of Africans who were able to take advantage of these changes.

Teaching Activities and Learning Outcomes

Assessment Opportunity

Explaining how and why interpretations differ.

Pupils will be able to
- explain reasons for migration
- identify similarities and differences between sources
- write a clear account reconciling information between different sources.

Starter

Source a on page 176 of *History in Progress – Book 3*, should be read out loud to the class and pupils asked to guess the speaker.

Development

Green task: Using **source a**, pupils should try and give reasons why people move. They might be asked to divide those reasons into push and pull factors. The reasons should be written down in full sentences.

Blue task: Working with a partner, each pupil should try and identify two or three points of similarity and two or three points of difference between **sources c** and **d** (page 177, History in Progress – Book 3). They should then compare their list with another pair.

Orange task: The task asks the pupils to write a summary article explaining how Barack Obama Sr. came from Africa to the USA. To write the article they should use the information from **sources a, c** and **d** (pages 176–177) selectively, attempting to reconcile the contrasting views as much as is possible. As part of the article, the pupils might be encouraged to explain why the evidence differs.

Plenary

Class discussion: Which source was more useful in finding out why Barack Obama Sr. moved to the USA; Why?

3.6a Where can migration lead?

3.6b A long road to the White House

Learning objectives
- To find out about Barack Obama's life.
- To explain diversity and change.

Historical background
After his victory in the presidential election in November 2008, Barack Obama was sworn in as the 44th President of the United States of America on 20 January 2009. Throughout his lifetime Obama has moved a number of times, for family, educational, vocational and political reasons. During his childhood he moved from Kenya to Indonesia and then to Hawaii. He studied in Los Angeles, New York and Cambridge Massachusetts before moving to Chicago for work. In 2009 he and his family took up residence in the White House in Washington DC.

Teaching Activities and Learning Outcomes

Assessment Opportunity

Explaining the extent of change.

Pupils will be able to

- place events in chronological order
- summarise why people move
- explain the positive impact of migration.

Starter

Working in pairs, pupils should try and identify some of the other events covered in the text book which were mentioned by Obama. How many events can the pupils identify?

Development

Green task: Pupils place the events onto a chronological timeline and write a 200 word summary at the end.

Blue task: In pairs, pupils identify the category for each of Obama's moves. They then discuss which category constitutes the most significant in his life.

Orange task: The task asks pupils to use the knowledge built up over the course about the impact of migration to answer the question. Pupils will probably need some advice as to how to best structure their work. They might also be given clues as to the areas to focus on (education, political opportunity, work).

Plenary

Class vote: Which move constitutes the most significant turning point of Obama's life?

Cross-curricular links

Citizenship: The American political system, opportunity, the question: when will the UK have a black Prime Minister?

Unit 3 Moving and travelling

3.7 Making connections: Why did people move around in the twentieth century?

Learning objectives
- To understand that moving and travelling involves journeys that are made for a multiplicity of reasons and that these differ between people within one mass movement as well as across time.
- To reflect upon the push and pull factors that have dominated the movement of people in the twentieth century.

Teaching Activities and Learning Outcomes

Assessment opportunity

The main thrust of this lesson lies in analysing motive. All the tasks provide an assessment opportunity for these particular skills. Two tasks have been set up as group work, so any assessment should take account of this and individual pupils' contributions must be able to be identified.

Starter

Quick-fire round the class: why did people move / travel in the twentieth century? Focus in on **sources a–d** on page 181 of *History in Progress – Book 3*. Move on to the green task.

Development

Green task: If time presses, this could be taken as a whole class plenary, ending with a whole class list of reasons for moving and travelling.

Blue task: Encourage discussion and the sharing of ideas. The grid supplied on **Worksheet 3.7** should help with sorting out and scoring the push and pull factors.

Orange task: There are two ways to hold the debate. The first is to do so formally: there will be a proposer and a seconder, as well as an opposer and a seconder making their speeches before opening the motion up to the floor. Alternatively, depending on the ability range of the pupils and time factors, there could simply be one pupil proposing the motion and another opposing it before letting the whole class give individual points of view.

NB. These tasks will take time if they are done thoroughly and pupils become absorbed. Ideally, this Making Connections section should be spread over two lessons.

Plenary

After final speeches in the debate, pupils vote on the motion. Is it carried or does it fall?

Cross-curricular links

English, Citizenship, Geography

Unit 3 Moving and travelling

Worksheet 3.7 Why did people move around in the twentieth century?

2 Look back over the enquiries we have dealt with in **Unit 3**. Working with a partner, use the table below to list the push and pull factors involved in the movement of people in each of the enquiries. Once you have listed the factors, score them on how important they were (5 is very important and 0 is not important at all).

Enquiry	Push factor?	Score	Pull factor?	Score

3 Which were the most important factors: push or pull? Explain your decision.

_____

_____

_____

_____

_____

Unit 3 Moving and Travelling

Assessment Unit 3

3.8 Assessment task 1: Why did people travel in the twentieth century?

Pupils will be able to

- evaluate source material in order to test an hypothesis
- weigh evidence and use it with factual knowledge in order to reach a supported judgement.

What the task is about

- The focus of this assessment task is hypothesis testing. Explain what an hypothesis is, and read out the one pupils are to test.
- Make sure pupils understand the four given sources, and talk through 'How will you set about a task like this?' on page 183 of *History in Progress – Book 3*.
- It is intended that pupils answer the questions on their own, using **Worksheet 3.8 (1)** as a guide if necessary. However, it is possible for pupils' findings to be taken as a whole class plenary before settling down to pull everything together in writing an answer to the question.
- Pupils move up the levels from Level 5 to 7 on the quality of their research and their writing up. A mark scheme is provided on **Worksheet 3.8 (2)**. Care must be taken if there was collaborative work; it will be necessary to identify the contribution of each pupil.
- This task should be undertaken at the end of the unit.

3.9 Assessment task 2: What was the most important movement of people in the twentieth century?

Pupils will be able to

- create and apply criteria to a decision making process
- present their findings to a specific target audience.

What the task is about

- The focus of this assessment task is creating material appropriate for use in a primary school. Explain to pupils that it is a development of **Assessment 1**.
- The first step is for pupils to write down the criteria against which they will judge the journeys made. Criteria might include, 'what was the impact on the people concerned?' 'What was the impact on the places they left?' 'What was the impact on the societies they joined?' 'Did their actions affect the way people live today?'
- Once the criteria have been selected, suggest to pupils that they apply this to the journeys taken and rate each criterion / journey on a scale of 1 to 5, where 5 is the most important. It might be helpful for pupils to complete **Worksheet 3.9 (1)**, which will help them in the decision-making process.
- Following that, pupils have to decide how they are going to present their findings. Remind them that they are producing work for children under the age of 11, and so it has to be lively and relatively simple.
- Pupils move up the levels from Level 5 to 7 depending on the quality of their reasoning criterion creation and the appropriateness of the outcome. The assessment task is designed so that there is differentiation by outcome. A mark scheme is provided on **Worksheet 3.9 (2)**. As the pupils are working in pairs, care must be taken that the contribution of each individual pupil can be recognised and assessed appropriately.
- This exercise should be undertaken at the end of the unit.

3 Moving and travelling

Unit 3 Assessment 1

Worksheet 3.8 (1) Why did people travel in the twentieth century?

What do the sources say?

Read **sources a–d** on pages 182–83 of *History in Progress – Book 3*. Make sure you understand them, research their context and make any possible links to fear.

Source	Summary of source content	Historical background (context)	Link to fear?
a			
b			
c			
d			

Can I trust the sources?

Now think about the provenance of the sources. What was the author / photographer in a position to know?

Source	Who created the source?	Points that show the creator is reliable	Points that show the creator is unreliable
a			
b			
c			
d			

How reliable are the sources as evidence of why people made journeys?

_____
_____
_____
_____
_____
_____

Now put all this information together to explain whether or not you agree with the hypothesis that people in the twentieth century only travelled because they were afraid.

3 Moving and travelling

Unit 3 Assessment 1

Worksheet 3.8 (2) Why did people travel in the twentieth century?

How did you do?

Level 5: I was able to ...

describe the reasons why people travelled in the twentieth century	
suggest how these reasons might be linked to fear	
begin to evaluate sources and establish links with fear	
select and use information, including the correct historical words to support and structure my work.	

Level 6: I was able to ...

explain how some reasons people travelled could be linked to fear, and how some could not	
evaluate sources to establish evidence for my enquiry	
select, organise and use information, including the correct historical words, to produce structured work and reach a judgement.	

Level 7: I was able to ...

analyse the reasons why people travelled in the twentieth century and link these to fear	
evaluate the evidence by considering, additionally, the provenance of the sources	
select, organise and use information, including the correct historical words, to produce structured work and reach a supported judgement	

Things I did well: _____

I need to learn more about: _____

One thing I could do to improve is: _____

I will do this by: _____

Pupil comment: _____

_____

_____

Teacher comment: _____

_____

Unit 3 Assessment 2

Worksheet 3.9 (1) What was the most important movement of people in the twentieth century?

These are the qualities (criterion) we have selected:

Criterion 1 _____

Criterion 2 _____

Criterion 3 _____

Criterion 4 _____

Criterion 5 _____

This is how we are ranking the criteria when applied to journeys

Journey	Criterion 1	Criterion 3	Criterion 4	Criterion 5	TOTAL

3 Moving and travelling

Unit 3 Assessment 2

Worksheet 3.9 (2) What was the most important movement of people in the twentieth century?

How did you do?

Level 5: I was able to …

describe the reasons for the journeys made by some people	
begin to ask questions about the importance of each journey	
select and use appropriate information in my presentation.	

Level 6: I was able to …

explain the reasons for the different journeys made	
ask questions that enabled me to decide why some journeys were more important than others	
select information relevant to the understanding of primary school children and use it in my presentation.	

Level 7: I was able to …

decide on the criteria to be used to judge importance	
explain how the criteria was used to determine the most important journey.	
select information relevant to the understanding of primary school children and use it in my presentation at the appropriate language level.	

Things I did well: _____

I need to learn more about: _____

One thing I could do to improve is: _____

I will do this by: _____

Pupil comment: _____

_____

_____

Teacher comment: _____

_____